SPRINGFIELD

SPRINGFIELD
AN INTIMATE PORTRAIT

KIMBERLY A. RINKER

AMERICA
THROUGH TIME®
ADDING COLOR TO AMERICAN HISTORY

America Through Time is an imprint of Fonthill Media LLC
www.through-time.com
office@through-time.com

Published by Arcadia Publishing by arrangement with Fonthill Media LLC
For all general information, please contact Arcadia Publishing:
Telephone: 843-853-2070
Fax: 843-853-0044
E-mail: sales@arcadiapublishing.com
For customer service and orders:
Toll-Free 1-888-313-2665

www.arcadiapublishing.com

First published 2020

ISBN 978-1-63499-220-6

Typeset in 10pt on 12pt Sabon
Printed and bound in England

Foreword

Growing up in Springfield, Ohio, offered what most youngsters in the Midwest are afforded: a loving family, a solid home base, hearty food, sports, and modest opportunities. After working in Chicago for thirty-one years, I returned to my hometown in 2015, and when given the opportunity to pen a historic title on an American city, Springfield was a natural choice. Learning about my hometown has enlightened me in ways I could not have imagined. It has been a fantastic ride thus far, so saddle up, grab the reins, and ride off as we explore a more intimate side of Springfield, Ohio.

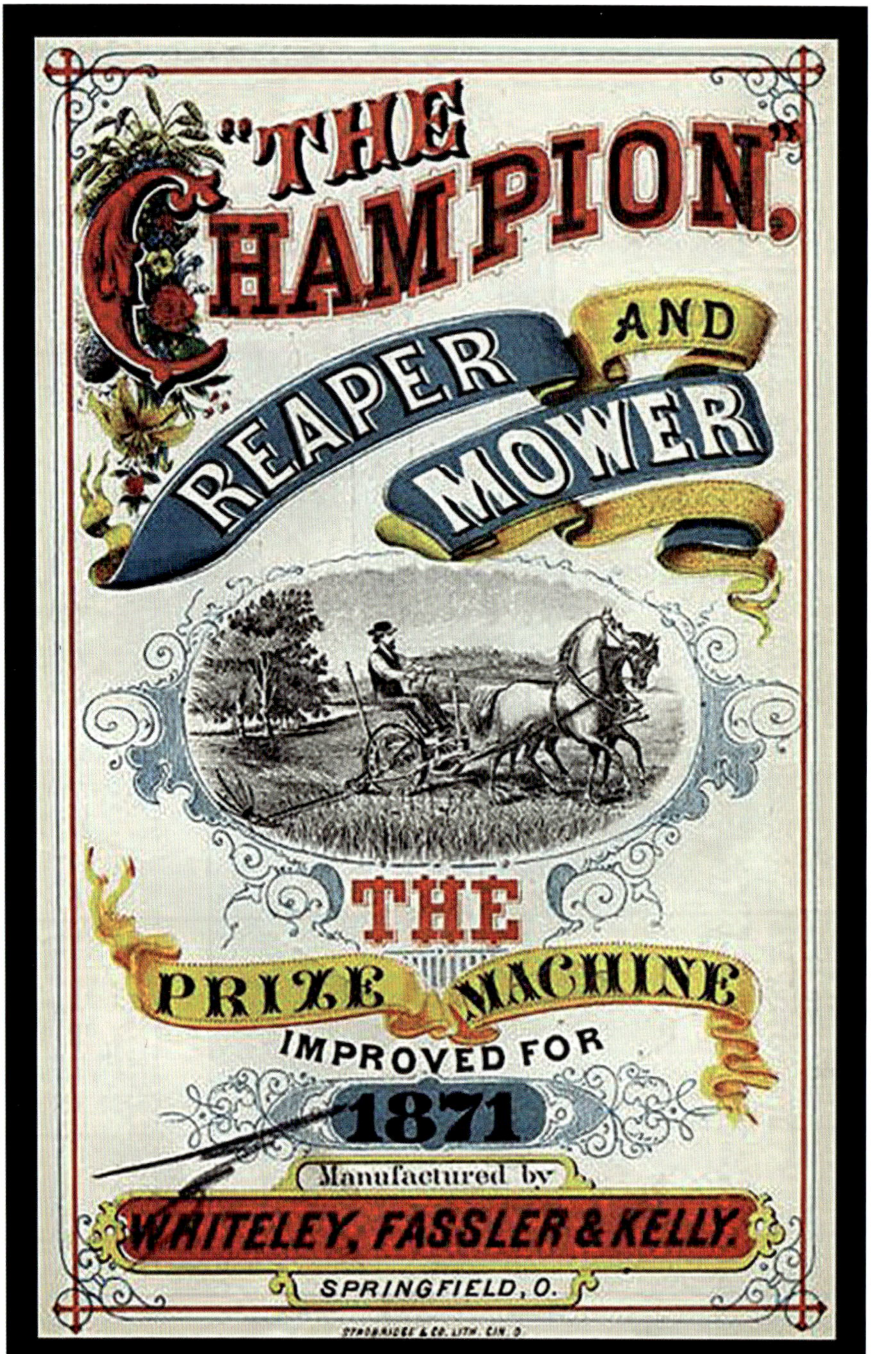

This Champion Reaper & Mower poster spouts the accomplishments of the Whiteley, Fassler & Kelly Company of Springfield in 1871. Their manufacturing company was first located on the southeast corner of High and Fountain Streets and eventually moved to the East Street Shops in 1883. (*Clark County Historical Society Archives)*

Contents

Lagonda Agricultural Works, Warder, Brokaw & Child poster from June 30, 1859. (*Clark County Historical Society Archives)*

Introduction

Much has been written of Springfield's history, from founder James Demint establishing the first city specs to Tecumseh, Madonna of the Trail, and Frank Lloyd Wright. While I will delve into some of those things, albeit briefly, in this book, my main objective is not to regurgitate news familiar to most local historians, but to enlighten readers with stories told by some of Springfield's most colorful citizens.

Springfield was once a pinnacle city, coined "Champion City" and "Rose City," among other monikers. Today, it retains a great portion of quintessential Americana, though no longer a major league player in commerce as it once was in the early part of the twentieth century. Yet, the congenial familiarity of its streets and residents remains.

1

The City at the End of the Road

The heart of Clark County was founded in 1801 by James Demint, who built the first cabin in 1799 where the Mad River and Buck Creek meet, on what would later become Springfield. The city rose out of the clutches of Kentucky settlers to become the county seat of Clark County, after the August 8, 1780 Battle of Piqua. Previously, this area had been home to the Peckuwe and Kispolo divisions of the Shawnee Indian Tribe. However, the 1795 Treaty of Greenville helped end most of the hostilities with the Native Americans who called Ohio home.

The first official Springfield census conducted in 1802 listed 510 residents—285 males and 225 females. The town was officially incorporated on January 23, 1827, and in April 1850, it was granted a charter by the state of Ohio. Four years later, the town had become a continuously growing enterprise of more than 10,000 citizens, offering everything they needed: proximity to streams and rivers, which allowed for a plethora of mills and factories to be erected, and ample prairieland suitable for farming.

Springfield had scored quick gains during the early and mid-nineteenth century in population via its location on the National Road, and from the influx of railroad lines that converged there. Ohio's first train service was the Mad River & Lake Erie Railroad, which came to Springfield on September 2, 1832 via the locomotive "Seneca."

The National Road's federal funds were cut short in 1839 and construction of the road came to a halt in Springfield in 1849, during which time the town was known as "The City at the End of the Road." Tiny schoolhouses popped up throughout Clark County, and by 1860, there were fifty public high schools in Ohio and more than 11,000 one-room schoolhouses in the Buckeye State.

Due to its agricultural resources, Springfield attracted inventors who produced reapers, threshers, mowers, and other farming implements. The moniker of "Champion City" was christened upon Springfield due to the Champion Reaper Crop Harvester Machine being manufactured on East Street. As well, reaper inventor Cyrus McCormick's son and Springfield native Benjamin Warder began the Lagonda Agricultural Works in 1840s, which morphed into International Harvester. In 1855, William Whiteley invented the mowing and reaping machine, and by 1880, his East Street plant was the second largest industrial facility under one roof in the world, second only to the Krupp Munitions Works in Prussia.

The City Brewery opened in 1849 on the corner of Penn and Section Streets, behind the current Schuler's Bakery on Main Street. City Brewery produced Blue Head Beer, and in 1890 merged with the Springfield Brewery, operating at this location until 1919, when prohibition was enacted state-wide. Citizens Dairy then took over the building on Penn Street Hill. *(Clark County Historical Society Archives)*

One of the first Hay Press Threshers manufactured by International Harvester, 1903. *(Clark County Historical Society Archives)*

Springfield became the largest producer of farm machinery from the Civil War through the first decade of the twentieth century. That changed in the early 1920s, when some of the larger manufacturers sold out to companies in Chicago and elsewhere, except for International Harvester, whose founders had deep-seated roots in Clark County.

Multiple churches were established in the mid-1800s of varying religious affiliations, with the Lutheran Church founding Wittenberg Seminary & College in 1845.

Industrialists such as Oliver S. Kelly, Asa Bushnell, James Leffel, and P. P. Mast would dominate Springfield's manufacturing resources. It was Bushnell who offered his Bushnell Building up to patent attorney Harry Aubrey Toulmin, Sr., who penned the 1904 patent on the airplane for Dayton brothers Orville and Wilbur Wright. Toulmin, Sr., a Springfield native, wrote five patents for the Wright brothers throughout the next several decades before his death in 1942.

In 1902, Springfield's Courthouse provided the venue for A. B. Graham, Springfield's superintendent of schools, to establish his "Boys and Girls Agricultural Club," later renamed "4-H." Eighty-five schoolchildren, ages ten to fifteen, were at that first meeting on January 15, 1902. The organization quickly blossomed into a nation-wide phenomenon, teaching children the importance of gardening, food preservation, and agricultural livestock and crop techniques. The four "H's" stand for "Head," "Heart," "Hands," and "Health," and that moniker continues to bear out Graham's vision some 118 years later, with more than 6 million youngsters in forty countries participating in 4-H today. Graham also established the first bookmobile to encourage rural-area children to read, utilizing an enclosed wagon pulled by horses.

In 1901, Springfield's population was 45,000. The city produced more manufactured goods in proportion to population than any other American city, and it manufactured more agricultural implants than any city in the world outside of Chicago. Springfield's 325 manufacturing plants had combined revenues of $18 million by 1905.

Springfield also had a healthy publishing business and strong automobile industry that blossomed in the beginning decades of the twentieth century. Names like Westcott, Bramwell, Breening, Chrysler, Dodge, and Kelly-Steam dominated the Springfield automobile arenas.

In 1919, Springfield was coined the "City of Roses" as it was home to thirty-three greenhouses, producing more roses than any other city in the world at the time. A total of 24 million roses were shipped to venues throughout the globe, as they were one of the city's top ten manufactured items, according to a 1928 city manager's report.

This ad for the Phineas P. Mast Cultivator appeared in a July 15, 1881 edition of the *Springfield Globe Republic*, on an inside page entitled "Mirror of Springfield's Manufacturing Industries." P. P. Mast was best known as a manufacturer of agricultural implements that included wind engines, pumps, lawnmowers, plows, and cultivators, among other inventions. Other manufacturers spotlighted on that page included James Driscol & Sons Carriages, Victory Corn Mill, Croft's Wind Engine, A. W. Eichelberger Cement, Drain & Sewer Pipes, Kenney & Minich's Champion Door Lip, Ludlow's Soap, J. J. Fawcett Champion Brass & Bell Foundry, St. John Sewing Machine Company, C. W. Wadsworth Sign Painter & Engraver, L. Patric Furnace, Springfield Threshing Machine Works, George Sintz's Stone Quarries & Lime Killers, T. B. Pett & Company Galvanized Cornice, Windows Caps & Finials, and Whiteley, Fassler & Kelly's Champion Harvesting Machines. (*Clark County Historical Society Archives*)

The Springfield Telegraph Office at 110 South Limestone Street in 1910. (*Clark County Historical Society Archives*)

Downtown Springfield, *circa* 1904. (*Clark County Historical Society Archives*)

Color postcard image of downtown Springfield on High Street, *circa* 1905, looking east from the middle of Fountain Square. The interurban train lines are clearly visible. (*Clark County Historical Society Archives*)

Postcard rendition of the Springfield Post Office, *circa* 1905. The post office was a convenient five-minute walk away from the Heaume Hotel. (*Clark County Historical Society Archives*)

The Sears Candy Counter in the late 1940s. Founded in 1886 in Minneapolis, the Sears & Roebuck Company opened its first store in Springfield in 1927 at 112 East Columbia Street before moving to East High Street in 1935. (*Clark County Historical Society Archives*)

Color postcard image of the Big Four Railroad Depot, 1910. (*Clark County Historical Society Archives*)

That same year, Springfield also ranked first nationally in the manufacturing of chicken incubators, brooders, and commercial thermometers via the Buckeye Incubator Company, which had been established in 1893 at 76 Euclid Avenue.

As the horse and buggy morphed into electric and gas-powered transportation, Springfield boasted streetcars and interurban lines that ran steadily until 1938. Railroad service continued to be strong into the fourth, fifth, and sixth decades with the "Big Four"—a stunning, state-of-the-art depot that was the heart of the city until 1969.

As of this writing, Springfield boasts a population of approximately 60,000, with 75 percent white, 18 percent African Americans, and the remainder a mixture of Hispanic, Asian, and other races living in the 412 square miles that make up Clark County.

The congenial assortment of races and personalities that encompass Springfield have, over the decades, produced standout professional sports figures, artists, musicians, authors, and visionaries. None is perhaps more well-known than John Legend, a North High School graduate who has gone on to become a Grammy and Oscar-winning singer-songwriter, philanthropist, and actor. Since North and South High schools merged in 2008 to become Springfield High School, the former South High School building and its famous dome are now host to the John Legend Theater and Career Connect Education Center.

Springfield native John Legend graced the May 1, 2017 cover of *Time* magazine, listing him as one of the nation's 100 Most Influential People. (*Author photo*)

2

ALL THE FITTING NEWS

One aspect of any burgeoning village, town, or city is reflected in the content of its local news. In the 1800s, the only source for local news came in the form of four- to eight-page tabloids. The first official newspaper published in Springfield was *The Farmer*, owned and started by George Smith in 1817 who sold it to Henry Rogers in 1820, who then renamed it the *Farmer's Advocate*. On December 18, 1824, Henry's brother, Simon, took over the paper and remained it *The Pioneer*, and in 1824, it became *The Western Pioneer*. In 1836, it became the *Springfield Pioneer*, and in 1849, publisher John M. Gallagher changed the name to *The Republic*, the first newspaper in the United States with that title. Smaller papers sprang up as either one- or two-page leaflets, but *The Republic* was the main source of regional and world news for the ever-growing town, and by 1872, it had a net stock worth of $125,000.

Another popular read was the *Leffel Mechanical News*. Established in March 1871, it was published monthly by James Leffel & Company at 50 cents for a subscription, with 30,000 to 35,000 copies sold monthly. The price increased to $1 for an annual subscription ten years later.

By 1881, the again-renamed *Springfield Globe-Republic* was an established eight-page daily that reported newsworthy items and ads alike on its front page.

By 1883, Springfield had 19,000 citizens and published nine newspapers, including *The Springfield Daily Republic* (evening newspaper); *The Gazette* (four pages, published Fridays); *The Live Patron* (eight pages, published Saturdays); *Springfielder Journal* (four pages, published Fridays in German); *The Transcript* (eight pages, published Fridays); *Farm & Fireside* (eight pages, published semi-monthly); *Grange Visitor* (thirty-two pages, published monthly); *Leffel's Illustrated Milling & Mechanical News* (eight pages, published monthly); and *The Wittenberger* (twenty pages, published monthly).[1]

The Wednesday, January 15, 1885 front page of the *Springfield Globe-Republic*, Vol. IV, No. 207, offered an ad for that day's readers with a list of goods and prices at the local markets: butter (20 cents); eggs (20 cents); oysters (25 cents per pound); rabbits ($1.25 per dozen); rice (8.5 cents per pound); potatoes (35–50 cents per bushel); and chickens (20–35 cents each).

Springfield Daily Republic.

VOLUME 27. SPRINGFIELD, OHIO: THURSDAY EVENING, JUNE 23, 1881. NUMBER 148.

BROWN.

CHEMICALLY PURE

PARIS GREEN

KILLING POTATO BUGS

40c Per Pound.

J. J. BROWN'S DRUG STORE

HATS AND CAPS.

New Mackinaws

Manilla Hats

GUGENHEIM'S.

HOME NEWS.

BY TELEGRAPH TO THE REPUBLIC.

BURTON.

BURTON'S NEW SODA FOUNTAIN

IS THE FINEST EVER BROUGHT HERE.

PURE FRUIT FLAVORING

Burton's Drug Store.

LUDLOW.

BRIGHAM'S

Aromatic Camphor

KILLS MOTHS.

PROTECT THEM THOROUGHLY.

25 cents per package.

CHARLES LUDLOW,

DRY GOODS.

NEW GOODS.

MURPHY & BRO.,

CORNER STORE,

DRESS GOODS.

DRY GOODS.

Barber, Willis & Co.,

Grand Central Store,

New and Elegant Novelties in Lace Articles,

BARR & CO.

BLANK BOOKS

Miscellaneous Books

50 TO 75 PER CENT. LESS

THAN REGULAR PRICE.

Above: The front page of the *Springfield Daily Republic*, June 23, 1881 shows the news of that Thursday. At the time, it was not uncommon to have ads appear alongside text on the front pages of these four- to eight-page newspapers. (*Clark County Historical Society Archives)*

Below: The Arcade Building—comprised of a hotel and shopping mall—was one of the city's main railroad stops. Charles Cregar of Springfield designed the building, which was described as having "a glass ceiling, with elegant business rooms on each side: with a fine ever-playing fountain in an open court in the center ... and the whole building is illuminated by the electric system. The structure has forty-seven business rooms, including Nelson's Business College, one of the roomiest, best lighted and most handsomely furnished colleges of its character in the country," by *The History of Manufactories of Springfield, Ohio* (1885). After being abandoned for several decades, the Arcade Building was destroyed in 1998. (*Clark County Historical Society Archives)*

Another headline from that same day read:

> Cheap Ocean Transports "The Red Star Steamship Line has issued circulars to its agents, giving the rate from Antwerp to New York and vice versa at $10. The Carr Line is also selling tickets at $10, and the Cunard Anchor and other English lines still adhere to the $15 fee for steerage passengers."

Springfielder Phineas P. Mast; his nephew and bicycle-seat inventor Thomas J. Kirkpatrick; and Kentucky-based printer John S. Crowell founded *Farm & Fireside* (1883–1950), a bi-monthly farm journal devoted to promoting Mast's agriculture products. Later, it focused on agricultural economics with a readership of more than half a million.

Mast, Crowell, and Kirkpatrick purchased *The Home Companion* as a sister publication to *Farm & Fireside*, and they changed the name to the *Ladies Home Companion* and later to *Women's Home Companion* (1883–1950). The publishing trio, reaping huge financial rewards of that latter publication, established their first printing headquarters at Wittenberg and High Streets.

Crowell—who became a major player in the Kelly-Springfield Motor Truck Company—bought out his partners in the late 1890s before selling the company in 1906 to Joseph Knapp and George Hazen. Knapp kept the Crowell name and added more magazines and books to the business, while Hazen ran the editorial side from his New York City office.

One of the company's most popular magazines was *The American*, purchased in 1911, which morphed from a muckraking tabloid into a popular magazine, carrying in-depth articles on global finance, human rights, and general interest. *Collier's: The National Weekly* was acquired in 1919 by the Crowell Publishing Company (incorporated January 31, 1906), and by 1924, its weekly circulation had grown to 1,250,000. That

Farmers stand with their then-modern plows made by Superior Farm Equipment and a trio of mule teams in the fields of Springfield, *circa* 1907. (*Clark County Historical Society Archives)*

A cover from *Collier's: The National Weekly*, January 21, 1922. (*Author's photo*)

year, *Collier's* publishing offices moved to Springfield, merging with Crowell, with a seven-building complex and 20 acres of floor space on West Main Street.

> Collier's is joining the group of magazines which have left New York in the last two or three years, principally because of conditions imposed by unions in the printing grades and beginning with the June 7 number, Collier's will be published in the plant of the Crowell Publishing Company at Springfield, Ohio.[2]

Peter F. Collier was born in County Carlow, Ireland, in 1849, and was educated there before moving to the United States, where he became a publisher of Roman Catholic books and novels, and later *Collier's Once A Week*, which he changed in 1895 to *Collier's Weekly: An Illustrated Journal*. When he died in New York City in 1909, his son, Robert, took over, becoming the weekly's editor in 1912. It was not until 1934 that Collier merged with Crowell and the company officially changed its name to Crowell-Collier Publishing Company.

Throughout the 1920s and 1930s, the countless assortment of magazines, books, and educational brochures helped to keep Crowell-Collier thriving through what otherwise would have been a tough time for the more than 2,000 workers employed at the Springfield complex.

By 1947, Crowell-Collier boasted 2,725 employees working daily at the eleven-building Springfield plant, but in the mid-1950s, heavy financial debts caused the company to suspend its three most popular magazines—including *Woman's Home Companion*, which boasted a monthly circulation of 9.3 million. In December 1956, the company discontinued all printing production and closed the Springfield plant. Crowell-Collier merged with Macmillan Company on May 6, 1965, and in 1973, the official title became Macmillan, Inc. The Springfield buildings were sold to Harry Denune in 1972, who established his Dixie Distributing Company there—a motorcycle parts business.

The Crowell-Collier partnership, in its heyday, boasted some of the finest journalists, photographers, authors, cartoonists, and literary agents of the twentieth century, including F. Scott Fitzgerald, Agatha Christie, Ansel Adams, Ernest Hemingway, Arthur Schlesinger, Jr., and Kurt Vonnegut, among others. The chronicles of its publications provide a solid reflection into the continuous shift of journalism from the first through the fifth decade of the 1900s.

Springfield's Only African American Newspaper

The Springfield Post was an African American newspaper that was published every Friday in 1956 for the price of 10 cents. The paper reflected all that was good and bad in the Springfield and national African American community at the time.

The Springfield Post emerged during the Civil Rights era, with front-page emphasis on national issues. It also had a lively social section, devoted to local marriage and birth announcements on the inside pages.

Owned by the Ben-Teau Publishing Company at 618 West Grand, *The Springfield Post*'s masthead offered: publisher and editor, B.P. Steptoe; associate editor, Tom Austin; women's editor and promotion director, Grace E. Lee; associated women's editor, Helen Arter; and circulation manager, Percy Lynes.

LATEST NATIONAL AND LOCAL NEWS

THE SPRINGFIELD POST

—SPRINGFIELD'S ONLY NEGRO NEWSPAPER—

THE VOICE OF SPRINGFIELD'S NEGROES

Price 10 cents

SPRINGFIELD, OHIO, THURSDAY, NOV. 22, 1956

Vol. 1, No. 43

LIMA, OHIO., WOMAN BEATEN TO DEATH

PARENTS FIND BODY IN BED SATURDAY

Home On Furlough

Moved By AME's To Cleveland

LAST MINUTE NEWS

ADA LEE STEALS BASIE SHOW

PATRONIZE OUR ADVERTISERS

LETTERS TO YE EDITOR

JOIN N.A.A.C.P. TODAY

Above: The front cover of *The Springfield Post* covered local, region, and national news pertinent to African Americans. (*Clark County Historical Society Archives*)

Opposite above: This cartoon appeared in the Thursday, July 19, 1956 edition of *The Springfield Post*. (*Clark County Historical Society Archives*)

Opposite below: The Springfield Post masthead from 1956. (*Clark County Historical Society Archives*)

Firm Leadership By The Government Would Convince Them

PAGE 2 SPRINGFIELD POST THURSDAY, MAY 17, 1956

THE SPRINGFIELD POST

NEWS, INFORMATION AND OPINIONS
PUBLISHED EVERY FRIDAY BY

The Ben-Teau Publishing Company

618 W. Grand FA. 3-9741

PUBLISHER & EDITOR .... **B. P. Steptoe**
ASSOCIATE EDITOR .... **THOMAS AUSTIN**
Woman's Editor and Promotion Director .... **GRACE E. LEE**
Associated Women's Editor .... **Helen Arter**
CIRCULATION MANAGER .... **Percy Lynes**

3

More Than a One-Horse Town

The Springfield Trotting Park was established at the west end of Springfield in 1882, and by 1901, it was a scene of gatherings and social outings in addition to the weekly harness races and horse shows contested on the grounds. The Ohio State Fair was held there in 1870 and 1871, before finding a permanent home in Columbus in 1886.

Later, during the first several decades of the twentieth century, Springfield's Clark County Fairground's half-mile oval was one of the state's top training tracks for harness horses, but the Great Depression and a devastating windstorm caused the fairgrounds to become abandoned.

Horseracing, boxing, and baseball were the most popular sports of the day, providing an outlet for folks struggling through hard times. Horseracing, especially, suffered during the first decade of the twentieth century when race-fixing and wagering scams prompted legislation to make all gambling illegal.

Nationwide, more than 300 racetracks had been whittled down to just twenty-five by 1910 and, likewise, many of the county fair ovals shut down their barn areas. That did not stop Springfield from being a hotspot on the national show scene, however, as many famous equines graced the fairgrounds during the first two decades of the twentieth century. Polo was a popular sport during those times as well.

During the early 1930s, legislators finally relented, seeing the opportunity for state-earned dollars by taxing horseracing. Upon reintroducing legalized wagering in 1933, once-closed tracks reopened, and new tracks sprang up across the nation to the delight of fans and horsemen alike. In the era before legalized sports wagering, opportunities to bet were limited to the racetracks. For those seeking to wager on baseball or boxing or other sports, the only opportunities came through local bookies.

Originally located on Springfield's west side, the fairgrounds—home of the Clark County Fair from 1853 through 1925—was near Pleasant Street and Western Avenue on Yellow Springs Street. That site later became Davey Moore Field in 1972. The half-mile oval was one of the best in the state, and the grandstand was a looming structure that could accommodate several thousands of spectators who flocked there to watch their favorite trotters and pacers vie on a summer afternoon. The stabling area included housing for several hundred Standardbreds, but when a water main broke at the head

Early pen drawing of the Springfield Trotting Park—where many horse activities took place, such as shows and races—from the early part of the twentieth century. (*Clark County Historical Society Archives*)

The Springfield Trotting Park, shown here in 1910, later morphed into the Clark County Fairgrounds. This image shows a trotter going a training mile near the rail of the half-mile oval near the judges' stand, while a gentleman at the left has just unhooked a team of horses from his two-wheeled sulky. Two horsemen stand at the left fence, while the grandstands loom boldly in the background. (*Clark County Historical Society Archives*)

Above: William McCulloch's & Sons retail shop featured horse and saddle goods as well as high-end luggage and catered to the equine elite community who converged upon Springfield for the numerous horse shows held in the first two decades of the twentieth century. Located at 40 East Main Street, McCulloch's sold trunks, harnesses, and boots for the avid horseman and foxhunter. *(Clark County Historical Society Archives)*

Opposite above left: The front page of the Sunday, June 11, 1916 *Springfield Daily News* reported that Springfield's eighth Annual Horse Show was slated for June 14, 15, and 16 and included many notable winners from the Madison Square Garden Show. "Ribbon winners of the East will compete with the winners of the West. Do not fail to attend. Boost Springfield and the Horse Show, which has a national reputation." General admission for the show was 50 cents and grandstand seats were 25 cents. A parking space for the three-day show was $15, and box seats—which accommodated ten people—were $25 to $45 for the three-day equine extravaganza. *(Clark County Historical Society Archives)*

Opposite above right: An inside page from the June 11, 1916 *Springfield Daily News* edition spotlighted two local harness horses—one a pacer and the other a trotter—who were slated to make their first starts of the season at a Monroe, Michigan, oval for Springfield-based trainer-drivers. *(Clark County Historical Society Archives)*

Opposite below: Horses were still the norm for transportation and farm work in the first two decades of the twentieth century in Springfield. In this photo from 1913, a member of the of the Longfellow family stands atop his wagon after harvesting hay. *(Clark County Historical Society Archives)*

THE SPRINGFIELD DAILY NEWS

[Sp]ringfield Horse Show Opens Wednesday at Clark County Fair Grounds; Few of Famous Steeds to be Exhibited at This Annual Event Pictured

KEY TO PICTURES

SPORTSMANSHIP IN SHOW RING IS ENCOUNTERED

Attitude of Noted Exhibitors is Above Reproach.

RIVALRY STIRS PUBLIC INTEREST

Judges of Springfield Event Will Have Well Known Trainers in Competition.

BY HAMILTON BUSBEY.

ZANESVILLE GIVEN CONVENTION AWARD

THE SPRINGFIELD DAILY NEWS

[O]F SEASON TO BE STAGED AT W[...]

THESE TWO LOCAL FLYERS TO MAKE THEIR FIRST START OF SEASON AT MONROE, MICH.

—Photos by Daily News.

Attention of local horsemen will be turned this week to the Monroe, Mich., meeting, which opens Tuesday, because Joe Ashland, the white pacer in Trainer Johnny Creamer's stable, and Grace Hussey, the consistent trotter, campaigned by Dick Shepherd, the popular trainer, will make their first start of the season there.

Joe Ashland, who is shown at the top, is scheduled to start in the 2:13 pace Tuesday, while Grace Hussey (at the bottom) will face the starter Wednesday in the 2:14 trot.

INDIANS BAT TWO PITCHERS OFF OF RUBBER

White Sox Defeat Washington When Pitcher Hits Batter With Bases Full.

Red Sox Stop Winning Streak of Fielder Jones' St. Louis Browns.

CLEVELAND, O., June 10.—Cleveland defeated Philadelphia 10 to 1 in the opening game of the series today hitting Pitchers Sheehan and Crowell hard. Speaker made five hits in as many times at bat, one being a double. He drove in two runs and scored three. Wyckoff, who finished the game for Philadelphia, was wild, but effective with men on, Cleveland having 12 men left on bases. Score:

Cleveland—	AB.	R.	H.	O.	A.
Graney, lf.	5	2	2	2	0
Turner, 3b.	4	0	0	3	2
Speaker, cf.	5	3	5	2	0
Smith, rf.	5	1	2	2	0
Gandil, 1b.	4	0	2	11	1
Howard, 2b.	5	0	2	0	2
Wambaganss, ss.	1	2	1	2	2
O'Neill, c.	4	1	2	3	0
Billings, c.	1	0	0	2	0
Coveleskie, p.	4	1	0	1	1
Totals	36	10	16	27	9

Philadelphia—	AB.	R.	H.	O.	A.
Witt, ss.	4	1	1	2	
Pick, 3b.	4	0	2	2	
Strunk, cf.	4	0	0	0	
Lajoie, 2b.	4	0	1	3	
McInnis, 1b.	4	0	1	9	
Walsh, rf.	4	0	0	1	
Oldring, lf.	4	0	0	3	
Meyers, c.	1	0	0	1	
Murphy, c.	3	0	1	2	
Sheehan, p.	0	0	0	0	
Crowell, p.	0	0	0	1	
Wyckoff, p.	2	0	2	0	
Totals	35	1	8	24	

Philadelphia.... 0 0 0 0 0 1 0 0 [...]
Cleveland...... 2 5 0 1 0 1 0 0 [...]

Two-base hits—Graney (2), Sp[eaker], Smith, Wambaganss, Pick, Mc[Innis], Witt. Sacrifice hits—Coveleskie, [Tur]ner, Wambaganss. Sacrifice fly—[Gan]dil. Double play—Pick to Laj[oie to] McInnis. Left on bases—Clevela[nd] [...]

of the stretch in 1936, it forced the many horsemen stabled there to relocate to nearby Urbana and London fairgrounds.

The fair was reinstated in August 1947 at the IOOF Farm Grounds, just south of Springfield on State Route 72, in conjunction with the 4-H Club Fair. In March 1948, the Clark County Commissioners purchased the 127-acre Springfield Municipal Airport grounds from the city for $35,000. The old hangers were kept and still provide a venue for 4-H projects and exhibitions.

In 1974, Springfield businessman Howard B. Noonan purchased 500 acres on Springfield's northwest side where he developed Windy Knoll Farm—which became one of the Buckeye state's top Thoroughbred breeding farms. Noonan, a Northwestern University graduate, was no stranger to the horseracing industry, having owned a share of 1971 Kentucky Derby winner Canonero II. He was also in partnership with Catesby W. Clay, owner of Kentucky's famed Runnymede Farm, and a longtime member and president of the Ohio Thoroughbred Breeders and Owners Board of Directors from 1981–1982.

Windy Knoll's state-of-the-art breeding facility included more than 20 miles of fencing that encased four stallion barns, four broodmare barns, and breeding sheds. The scarlet and gray barns melded perfectly on to the idyllic setting between Routes 68 and 72. In its heyday, Windy Knoll was home to more than 100 head of livestock, standing eight stallions. Some of his top racehorses included Sirland, an Irish-bred racer who was second to Affirmed in the $500,000 Hollywood Gold Cup, on the day the latter became racing's first $2 million earner. Other top earners included Terrible Tiger, Star of Kuwait, Sir Dragonet, Spirit Son, and Bobby Mercer.

Noonan bred many top horses at Windy Knoll including Air Forbes Won and Execution's Reason, the latter whom he also owned. The son of Executioner was foaled on May 3, 1977 at Windy Knoll and won his first four starts at Chicago's Arlington Park in 1979, including the Grade 1 Arlington-Washington Futurity. Racing through age six, Execution's Reason amassed a record of eight wins, seven seconds, and six thirds in thirty-six career starts with a $178,504 bankroll.

Air Forbes Won was a 1979 son of Bold Forbes that Noonan sold for $50,000 at the 1980 Keeneland July Selected Yearling Sale. The colt earned $237,700 with triumphs in the Grade 1 Wood Memorial and Grade 2 Gotham Stakes before finishing a disappointing seventh in the 1982 Grade 1 Kentucky Derby. Noonan died on December 22, 1982 at the age of seventy-four, and part of his land was purchased by investors and revamped into Windy Knoll Golf Club.

SPRINGFIELD DAILY NEWS

FINAL EDITION

WORLD-WIDE NEWS COVERAGE BY THE ASSOCIATED PRESS

SPRINGFIELD, OHIO, WEDNESDAY, AUGUST 18, 1948.

26 PAGES

FIVE CENTS

Fails to Dampen Optimistic Hopes of Exhibitors

Old Municipal Airport Site Takes On That 'New Look'

Mild Weather Promised For County Fair

Displays Housed In 225 Tents

Truman Congressional Attacks Cause Disagreement Among

Governor Denies Pleas To Block

$500,000 Blaze Destroys Piqua's

The Wednesday, August 18, 1948 *Springfield Daily News* touted the new Clark County Fairgrounds. (*Clark County Historical Society Archives)*

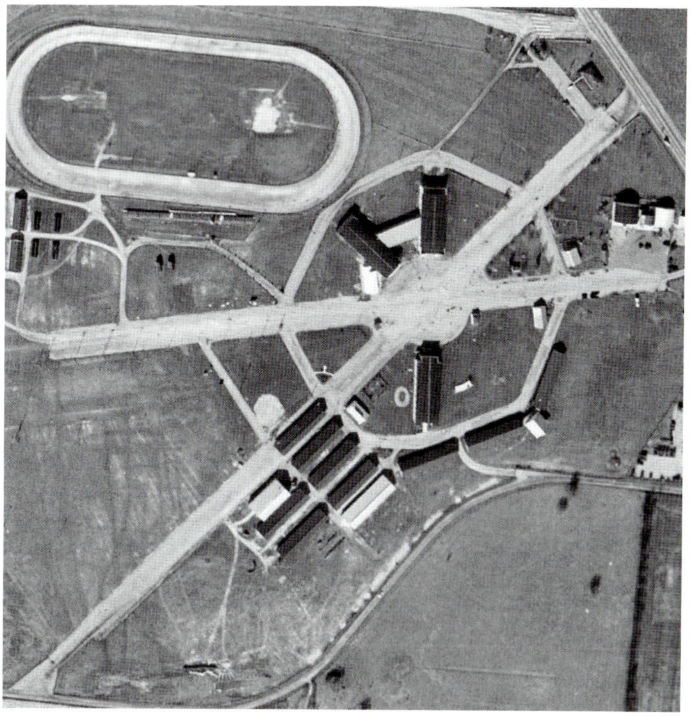

An aerial view of the Clark County Fairgrounds in 1959, featuring the old hangers and half-mile harness racing oval. (*Clark County Historical Society Archives)*

4

Racial Tensions

Like many American cities, Springfield has had its share of racial conflicts. In late February 1904, a white police officer was killed by an African American man named Richard Dixon in an area along the Mad River known as the Levee. Dixon was arrested and taken to jail. A short while later, a mob formed, swarmed the jail, dragged Dixon from his cell, and lynched him in a public square. The mob then attacked the Levee district, setting fires to African American-run bars, gambling dens, and prostitution parlors, as well as to homes occupied by African Americans.

The madness did not stop there. Two years later, a mob attacked the Levee businesses and homes again, not long after those living there had rebuilt what the mob had destroyed in 1904. The destruction to the area was catastrophic and surprisingly not unique to Springfield or other cities in the North during that era.

> The militia has been called out to check a race riot caused by the shooting of M. M. Davis, a brakeman, by a negro. A mob of 2,000 men, led by railroad men, descended tonight on the negro quarter of the town. They burned buildings and attacked all the colored men that ventured on the streets. Kempler's Saloon, on East Columbia Street, was the first object of attack. Major Horace Keifer called on the two local companies of militia to aid in restoring order, and the Xenia Company was ordered to report at a moment's notice. Three companies of the National Guard were called out.[1]

What makes this kind of violence difficult to comprehend is that Ohio was a major player in the abolitionist movement, with hundreds of Underground Railroad stations and "a network of roads, safe houses and churches through which runaway slaves escaped to their freedom," according to author Marilyn K. Howard in *Black Lynching in the Promised Land: Mob Violence in Ohio, 1877–1916*. Howard surmises that lynching and militia involvement were most likely to take place in Ohio's Clark and Champaign counties during this era based on the theories of historian Roberta Senechal de la Roche, who argues that near elimination of Ohio lynchings after 1916 came because of the 1896 anti-lynching bill.

"Ohio was beginning to develop a reputation for lawlessness that led to embarrassing comparisons to the South," Howard wrote, stating that, "Finally, although some whites

Springfield was home to the 9th Battalion of the Ohio National Guard Band in 1900. (*Clark County Historical Society Archives)*

visited the bars and brothels in the black neighborhoods of Springfield, Ohio, segregation was the rule," and "these little known lynchings and averted lynchings in Ohio show us that race hatred and mob violence against blacks was not solely a southern phenomenon."

In May 1912, both presidents William H. Taft and Teddy Roosevelt spoke in a tabernacle that former baseball star Billy Sunday had built after he became a minister. Springfield's African American community—at first excited at the prospect of hearing the two politicians speak—soon became part of a heated debate focused on race.

However, the racial tensions that were so prominent in the South had affected Springfield in various ways far before the twentieth century. In 1887, a state statue required that all schools allow white and black children to attend the same schools, attempting to end to segregation. This prompted the firing of many African American teachers throughout the state, including those in Springfield.

The Dilbert Avenue School—located at Dilbert and Jackson Streets—and later renamed Fulton School, began in 1884 and was one such school that suffered racial discrimination. Despite attempts in 1898 by a group of African American teachers to create an all-black school, the Springfield School Board thwarted those hopes and Springfield schools continued to prevent the hiring of African American teachers.

It was not until after World War I that African American teachers and community leaders began to garner support for an all-black elementary school that would employ African American teachers. This happened largely through the efforts of Hattie Mosely, who, according to the Springfield Historical Society, "came from Georgia in the 1920s and quickly became very active in the effort to break down Springfield's color barrier."

The Springfield Dilbert School 1902. (*Clark County Historical Society Archives*)

The Ku Klux Klan marches through Springfield in 1923. (*Clark County Historical Society Archives*)

Finally, on May 22, 1922, the Springfield School Board voted two-to-three to designate Fulton School as an all-black elementary school, with twelve African American teachers employed along with Principal R. W. Bullock. However, this decision by the school board was unpopular within both the white and black population, and locals began picketing the school daily.

The result was that school attendance rarely topped out at fifty students, nearly 200 less than the number of African American children assigned to attend. Later, it was discovered that the superintendent and many members of the school board were members of the Ku Klux Klan, and even after the superintendent's resignation, Fulton School continued to be a source of consternation between the black and white communities. A new superintendent promptly fired all the Fulton School teachers, promising to rehire them if Fulton opened as an all-black school. Ultimately, the school reopened and white teachers were hired to teach the attending African American children.

Gasoline Alley

To further understand that era's mindset, an examination of other societal aspects—specifically cartoons in the daily papers—offers insight. *Gasoline Alley* is one of the longest running comics in newspaper history, second only to *The Katzenjammer Kids*. Created by Tomah, Wisconsin, native Frank King, the strip debuted on November 24, 1918 in the *Chicago Tribune*. It appeared in the Springfield newspapers for more than four decades and introduced characters who evolved in both situations and age over the years, making it one of the most innovative comics. After its *Tribune* debut, it was picked up by many national publications, including the Springfield papers.

The comic's most popular characters included "Skeezix" and a maid named Rachel. King, in creating Rachel, epitomized the stereotypical portrait of African Americans by many whites at the time. The conundrum in King's depiction of Rachel lies in that she is a strong character, and by no means demoted in terms of her role within the comic. Clearly, King's depiction of the African American characters in both looks and manner of speaking is offensive but also indicative of public acceptance of such portrayals at the time.

> King was clearly drawing from the longstanding "Mammy" stereotype in creating her, but she also emerges as a very strong independent character in her own right. As a white American born in 1883, King shared in the widespread racism of the era: he used the n-word on at least one occasion in his correspondence and in a comic strip. He often portrayed blacks with a bemused condescension.[2]

King wrote:

> The fact that while going to school (in Chicago) I got a job running an elevator, furnished me with Rachel for the strip. Ten cents for a can of beer on Saturday night insured me a generous chicken dinner on Sunday and gave me entry to the kitchen where Rachel presided; big, black and jovial.

The cartoon strip *Gasoline Alley* was one of the most popular comics in the Springfield papers in the 1930s. *(Clark County Historical Society Archives)*

Obviously, King had affection for Rachel and created a relatable and overtly strong character who transcended his own personal awareness of racism and bigotry. What made the strip popular with readers was King's use of humor in relatable family situations in small-town America. Sadly, it is apparent from perusal of newspapers that Springfield was not immune to the era's racial stereotypes in print, movies, and radio. Despite these tainted portrayals, many of the African Americans who grew up in Springfield in the twentieth century forged above and beyond the bigoted ways of others to emerge as strong examples of the American Dream.

Prominent African Americans

One of Springfield's first African Americans who rose to national prominence was Robert Clayton Henry, born July 16, 1921 to Guy and Nellie Reed Henry. After attending Wittenberg University and the Cleveland College of Mortuary Science, he opened the Robert C. Henry Funeral Home in 1951 in Springfield. Henry began his foray into political circles as a member of Springfield's city commission in 1962 and was appointed by the commission as mayor of Springfield in 1966—the first African American mayor in the United States—serving through 1968.

Henry followed in the footsteps of the city's first Jewish mayor, Maurice K. Baach. He chose not to run for a second term and was succeeded by Springfield's first female mayor Betty Brunk, maintaining his seat on the commission. Henry was then selected by President Lyndon B. Johnson to serve on a Vietnam fact-finding commission and worked under President Richard Nixon as well. A member of the Republican Party, Henry was the nominee for the 60th District seat in the Ohio House of Representatives in 1972 but lost the general election. He died in 1981 and is buried in Ferncliff Cemetery.

Wayne Richard Embry is another Springfield native who overcame the racial prejudice of his home city to become a nationally recognized citizen. Growing up on his parent's 24-acre farm on Route 41, just west of where the Upper Valley Mall stands in an area known as "The Hill," was often tough, as Embry describes in his book, *The Inside Game*: "Because of the social situation at the time, we were more or less confined to The Hill or the surrounding neighborhood. We could not go to movies or eat in restaurants." Embry wrote:

> Joe Lewis was a hero to millions of black folks. Here was a black man who could beat up a white man and not only not get in trouble for it but get paid big money to do it. He represented all of us who took abuse from whites and did not fight back because of the fear of lynching, unfair arrest, and further exclusion from mainstream society. We lived vicariously through him.

Solid family values and a disciplined work ethic helped escalate Embry to NBA prominence. He would play eleven years in the NBA for three teams—the Milwaukee Bucks, Cincinnati Royals, and Boston Celtics—after graduating from Miami University in 1958, and he ranks twelfth all-time in scoring with 1,401 points and second in rebounds with 1,117 boards and five All-Star Teams performances. He is a member of the Miami Hall of Fame (1970), College Basketball Hall of Fame (2006), and Naismith Hall of Fame (1999).

Embry was the first African American general manager (for the Milwaukee Bucks in 1972) and team president in NBA history, and he was named NBA Executive of the Year in 1992 and 1998. Today, Embry serves as the advisor to the Toronto Raptors.

Above left: Wayne Embry, who grew up on the west side of Springfield, rose to prominence as a National Basketball Association (NBA) player and was the first African American to be a general manager of an NBA team—for the 1972 Milwaukee Bucks. (*Photo courtesy of Don Rinker*)

Above right: Wayne Embry, ever popular, has a road named after him in Springfield. (*Clark County Historical Society Archives*)

Another family who emerged unaffected by Springfield's racial tensions was the Ayers Family. Frank and Betty Ayers raised eight children on June Street, and all went on to success no matter what endeavor they chose, with Randy and Tim the two most prominent members of the family.

Randy (aged sixty-four) was named Ohio AAA 1974 Player of the Year and later obtained his BA (1978) and MA (1981) in education. He was a third-round NBA draft pick by the Chicago Bulls in 1978, and he then coached at Miami of Ohio before becoming Ohio State's basketball coach in 1989, earning 1991 National Coach of the Year and 1991 & 1992 Big Ten Coach of the Year titles. On June 20, 2003, he was named head coach of the Philadelphia 76ers, and in 2013, he was inducted into the Ohio Basketball Hall of Fame. He has been a scout for the Brooklyn Nets since 2015 after serving as the New Orleans Pelicans' lead assistant coach.

Tim Ayers (born November 19, 1958) was the sixth child and became a prominent member of both local and state government. Serving as Springfield's mayor from 1984 to 1990, he had been an assistant clerk in the Ohio House of Representatives from 1980 to 1984, and a special assistant, Ohio Department of Agriculture, during Governor Richard Celeste's administration. Currently, he serves as executive director of West Lakes Partnership, an organization that works to create economic opportunities for residents of an Orlando, Florida, suburb.

One of the most well-known musicians in the world, Johnny Legend needs no introduction. Born John Roger Stephens on December 28, 1978 to Phyllis and Ronald Stephens of Springfield, Legend was homeschooled by his mother while his father worked at International Harvester. He began singing with his church choir at the age of four and began playing the piano at seven. After graduating from North High School at the age of sixteen, he attended the University of Pennsylvania, studying English and African American literature. There, he directed the *a cappella* group Counterparts and graduated with honors in 1999 before moving to New York City where he quickly gained a faithful fan base. From there, his career took off and decades later he is one of the most sought-after musicians in the world, with ten Grammys, an Oscar, a Tony, and numerous other awards rewarding his talent. In total to date, Legend has won twenty-five awards from seventy nominations.

5

Public Enemy Number One

Public Enemy Number One is no stranger to American criminal history. John Dillinger's frequent visits to Ohio from his home state of Indiana afforded him both convenience and ease of movement within the Buckeye State, where he was feared and admired by both the public and law enforcement alike.

Dillinger committed his first bank robbery at the New Carlisle National Bank, located on the southeast corner of Routes 235 and 571 on Springfield's western edge, where he stole $10,600 on June 21, 1933.[1] He was just thirty years old at the time, and a few nights before the robbery, he had holed up in the Bancroft Hotel in Springfield. Later, upon similar visits to the Clark County area, Dillinger would stay in a house on Cedar Street.

"As kids, we'd walk by the Cedar Street house where Dillinger was hold up, when we heard he was in town," noted Don Rinker, a Springfield native and long-time resident who was raised at 426 Cedar Street. "It was kind of known in the neighborhood when he was there and not to go near the house, but as kids, we thought it was kind of exciting to have a bank robber so close—especially one as famous as Dillinger. We'd shuffle by there and whisper and try not to be seen glancing up at the house to see if we might see Dillinger peeking out the windows."

The house at 513 Cedar Street, located between Lannert Avenue and Plum Street (just west of Springfield Hospital), played host to Dillinger on more than one occasion, Rinker remembered.

"It was a fairly good-sized house," Don said. "There were two apartments on the bottom and one on the second floor. We walked by it every day on the way to school. I was just six the year he robbed the New Carlisle Bank, but I remember the talk about it and in later years, hearing whispers that Dillinger was hold up there again."

Prior to coming into Springfield that first time, Dillinger and three disciples—Paul "Lefty" Parker, William Shaw, and Noble Claycomb—had stopped at a hardware store on the outskirts of Springfield owned by Joe Wilcox, and they purchased two large bags of roofing nails.[2] After the robbery, with Dillinger driving as they sped away, his two henchmen dropped nails out of each side of the Hudson Terraplane to foil any police officer's pursuit.

Springfield lore says that local cops knew Dillinger was staked out at the Bancroft Hotel and were so afraid of him that they hid all night in the nearby Ohio Theatre. As well, Dillinger's historic first robbery was especially unfortunate for Wilcox, as he was chairman of the board of the New Carlisle Bank and its largest stockholder.

Dillinger returned in September and was captured in a Dayton boarding house on 324 West First Street. Four pistols, $2,600 in cash, quantities of rifle and shotgun shells, detailed notes explaining the speediest ways to escape from various cities, and sacks full of carpet tacks were found in Dillinger's possession at the time of his arrest.[3]

One of the reasons that Dillinger—even though he spent time in Springfield—and others like him of the day such as "Baby Face" Nelson and "Pretty Boy" Floyd never attempted to rob a Springfield bank was because of the Big Four Depot. More than fifty freight and passenger trains arrived daily at the Big Four and road traffic in and out of Springfield was frequently blocked by the number of trains and railway stops. Therefore, a criminal could not count on a quick escape from the track-lined town.

The First National Bank of New Carlisle, located on Springfield's far west side, was the site of gangster John Dillinger's first robbery on June 21, 1933. (*Clark County Historical Society Archives)*

6

Banker's Scandal

Asa Smith Bushnell was born in Rome, New York, on September 16, 1834, and moved to Springfield in 1851 when he was seventeen years old. Though his family was involved in the Underground Railroad, Bushnell was more interested in traditional businesses, working first as a dry goods clerk before becoming a bookkeeper for Leffel, Cook and Blakeney in 1857. Six years after settling in Springfield, Bushnell married Ellen Ludlow, daughter of Springfield pioneer and businessman John Ludlow. In 1867, Bushnell became part of a start-up a reaper and mower company that would garner him great wealth.

During the Civil War, Bushnell was a captain of a 100-man infantry in the Shenandoah Valley, but maintained his businesses, and at the war's end, he was a prominent member of the Springfield community. He was president of the First National Bank of Springfield and the Springfield Gas Company, with financial interests in the city's telephone and urban streetcars. He was named president of the Warder, Bushnell and Glessner Company, which later morphed into International Harvester.

Bushnell was also involved in politics, working for the Republican Party and helping to elect Joseph Foraker as Ohio Governor in 1885. Ten years later, Foraker returned the favor, helping Bushnell to secure the nomination for governor and eventually besting James E. Campbell for the top spot in 1896, winning by 92,622 votes as Ohio's fortieth governor and following in the footsteps of William McKinley. He was reelected in 1898 to a second term and sent the first volunteer units from Ohio to fight in the Spanish-American War.

Upon leaving the governorship in 1900, Bushnell focused his efforts on his business, concentrating on the interurban railway system. The Bushnell home, located at 838 East High Street, was built in an affluent neighborhood and is on the National Register of Historic Places.

Bushnell passed away on January 15, 1904 at the age of sixty-nine and was buried in Springfield's Ferncliff Cemetery. He had divvied up $750,000 between his family members just two weeks before his death.[1]

Bushnell had two daughters and a son, John L. Bushnell, who took over the family's business interests prior to his father's death, including as president of both the First National Bank of Springfield and American Trust and Saving Bank of Springfield, along with serving as president of Champion Construction and the Springfield, Troy & Piqua Railroad. John L. was born on February 15, 1872, and after graduating from Princeton University in 1894, he returned to Springfield where he married Jessie M. Harwood and had two sons, Asa A. and Edward H., and a daughter, Suzanne. He was a terrific horse enthusiast and president of the Springfield Horse Show.

Sometime in late 1918 or 1919, John L. had an affair with Rose Putnam—a Brattleboro, Vermont, native, wannabe Hollywood starlet, and West Coast socialite with a long history of affairs with wealthy older men. John L. (aged forty-six) hooked up with Rose on a chance meeting in Boston. John L. frequented the elite horse show circuits of the day, hob-knobbing with the Asters, DuPonts, and Vanderbilts. He served on the board of directors of New York's National Horse Show, one of the most prestigious equine competitions in North America as his horses were some of the best show ponies around—top driving and saddle equine athletes such as The Governor, June Maid, Queen Welcome, and Lady Jessie, among others.

After their initial meeting, John L. invited Rose to accompany him to the races at the Fair Grounds in New Orleans, sending her $100 to purchase a first-class train ticket. Working at Hamburger's Department Store in Los Angeles, Rose made the journey to Beamont, Texas, where she and John L. spent the night before heading to New Orleans. Registering as Mr. and Mrs. John L. Bushnell at the Gruenwald Hotel, the couple enjoyed the races and spent their evenings dancing and drinking at the Gruenwald's infamous Cave Nightclub.

Rose's uncle—an equally unsuccessful actor named Donald Osborn (aged twenty-eight)—encouraged his young niece to keep the affair going and, along with a petty Hollywood criminal named Blackie Madsen (aged fifty, real name Ross G. Sheridan), conjured up a scheme to extort money from Bushnell.

On December 4, 1922, Osborn and Madsen arrived in Springfield from Los Angeles via Chicago, with Osborn registering at the Shawnee Hotel at Main and Limestone and Madsen at the Arcade Hotel on High and Fountain. Both listed their address as 2575 Beachwood Drive, Hollywood, California. The Shawnee was located just a block from the Bushnell Building where the First National Bank was housed on the ground floor.

Osborn procured a meeting with John L., telling him he was Rose's brother and that federal agents were holding Rose in Lima, Ohio, and that they had been followed since leaving California. Osborn threatened John L. with the Mann Act, also known as the White Slave Traffic Act, enacted June 25, 1910 to "prohibit interstate transport of any woman or girl for the purpose of prostitution or debauchery, or for any other for immoral purpose" by Illinois Congressman James R. Mann. The letters the agents had, which gave proof of John L. paying for Rose to travel across state lines, were damning evidence.

Shaken, John L. met with Osborn and Madsen the next day, producing the $10,000 in exchange for the love letters. Madsen, who introduced himself as "Special Agent Robbins," wore a "United States Department of Justice" badge and John L., suspicious, grilled him repeatedly. After a series of heated verbal exchanges, the men parted company.

In early spring 1923, John L. received a letter from Californian Fred Moore, a bit actor who had overheard Osborn and Madsen bragging about the con they had pulled on Bushnell. Moore used an alias (Earl Frank Dustin) for safety and assured John L. in his letter that patience would be the key to catching the blackmailers. Bushnell did not have long to wait.

The Arcade Hotel during the time of the attempted blackmail of Springfield banker and wealthy businessman John L. Bushnell. *(Clark County Historical Society Archives)*

On July 10, 1923, Rose and Osborn were waiting for John L. when he came to work. When the pair demanded $100,000 from the banker, John L. suggested they return later that afternoon to give him time to amass the funds, and they acquiesced. Madsen, who was staying at the Shawnee Hotel, grew suspicious and he and fellow criminal, Chicagoan John A. Ryan, along with Rose, decided not to return to the bank with Osborne.

Later, when Osborne arrived at the First National Bank, he found John L. and Nicholas Fischer, who claimed to be a private investigator, waiting for him. It was not long before Osborn was in handcuffs after "Detective" Fischer asked him a series of questions he failed to answer. FBI agents were waiting for Osborn at police headquarters who told them where his co-conspirators were staying. However, Madsen and Ryan had fled, leaving Rose to fend for herself; she was arrested the following morning.

Rose and Osborne were taken to serve time in the Troy, Ohio, jail, and were arraigned on charges of extortion.[2] Standing before United States District Judge Smith Hickenlooper, Osborne was sentenced to serve twenty-one months in the Federal Penitentiary at Atlanta, Georgia, while Rose was sentenced to serve six more months at Troy. Attorneys John M. Cole of Springfield and Andrew Iddings of Dayton represented Bushnell.[3]

The actual letters in question were not presented as evidence until March 7, 1924, when a new blackmailer, Lawrence McClean, was arrested by police as a burglary suspect and confessed. In the meantime, Madsen had been arrested in Los Angeles and sent to Cincinnati to stand trial, while John A. Ryan was arrested just twenty-one days later, and the matter was finally put to bed.[4]

7

Cedar Street Memories

Donald "Spanky" Rinker was born on August 8, 1927 to Opal and Horace Rinker, living first on Schaffer Street on Springfield's south side and later, on the now defunct area of Cedar Street, west of Plum Street. Along with his sisters, Ruby and Maxine, Rinker roamed the neighborhood and quickly found out the importance of earning a buck.

"My dad [Horace Rinker] worked for Fout's Candy Company and later drove a truck for a living and had a shop in his garage where he would work on his race cars," Don related. "He was into race cars similar to today's Indy cars. They raced around the smaller towns on dirt tracks. Dad owned a car with a fellow named Phil Melaney who was a driver and a good friend."

Don was and still is known to many in Springfield as "Spanky" for his childhood resemblance to Spanky McFarland of *Little Rascals*' fame. His mother, Opal (French) Rinker, worked at the Crowell-Collier plant during World War I and at a Cedar Street grocery store.

Don explained:

> There were no big supermarkets in Springfield then. For instance, in our neighborhood there were three small grocery stores: one on Cedar, another on North Street and one on Race Street. Everybody knew everybody else's families and kids became friends because we all walked to Snyder Park Junior High School together every morning, which was about a mile from the neighborhood.

Don quickly became friends with many in the neighborhood, including Harry Amato, who would later pitch for the Pittsburg Pirates. The two became pals early in life when they both attended Western Elementary School, located on Main and Yellow Springs Streets. Don noted:

> Harry Amato and I played on the Snyder Park junior high football team. I was a lineman and he was the whole team—the quarterback and running back—as we

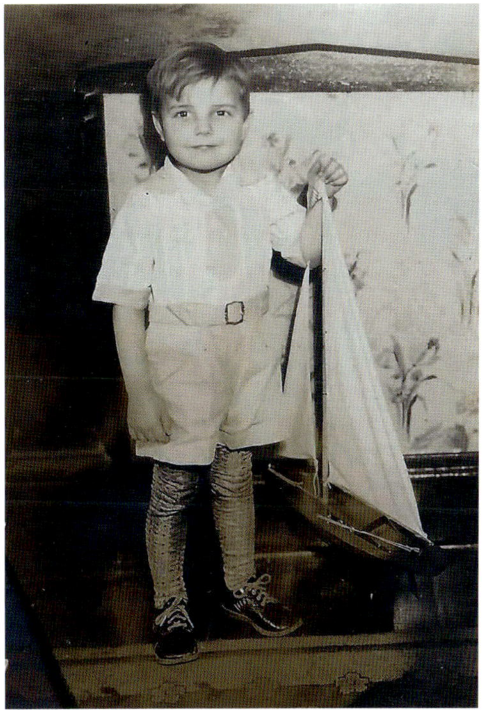

Right: Don "Spanky" Rinker, four years old, Springfield, Ohio, August 8, 1931. (*Don Rinker photo*)

Below: The Fout Candy Company was founded in 1889 by William H. Pretzman and Stillie T. Fout. The pair opened their first retail outlet at 40 South Fountain Avenue. When Pretzman left the business in 1905, Fout partnered with Albert L. Seitz and moved the store to 23 East Main Street and then to 11 North Fountain. The factory was located at 508 West Main Street. Don Rinker's father, Horace Rinker (far right), and his brother-in-law, Howard French (far left), stand inside the factory in June 1922. (*Clark County Historical Society Archives)*

Above: This photo from October 26, 1930 shows race car driver Phil Melaney, who partnered with Don Rinker's father, Horace Rinker, in owning and racing cars during that era. (*Don Rinker photo*)

Below: Longo's Fruit Market, 1925, was one of Springfield's neighborhood grocery stores, located on Main Street near Wittenberg Avenue. (*Clark County Historical Society Archives)*

> only played six-man football then. It was the only year Snyder Park won the city championship. Harry was the best football player in the city and Springfield High School wanted him to play for them, but he was also playing for the American Legion team and that's when he got a call from the Pittsburg Pirates. He signed with them at age 17. He was a heck of an athlete.

Don continued:

> He could really hit a baseball. The coaches made him hit right-handed because he would hit the balls so hard that he'd break windows out of the auditorium that was in right field. But he'd look around at recess, and if no teachers were on duty, he'd hit left-handed and break all kinds of windows out of the auditorium.
>
> We used to steal watermelons down at Bob Smith's fruit market and one of the kids would crawl up there and push a watermelon down and roll it to Harry because he could run faster than anyone else. So he'd take off running with it. We didn't have any money back then, so a watermelon was a real treat.

Amato was just seventeen years old when he signed with the Pittsburg Pirates on October 7, 1943, as the *New Castle, Pennsylvania News* reported: "The Pittsburg Pirates today signed a 17-year-old Ohio American Legion outfield for Spring delivery. The new

A young "Spanky" Rinker who grew up playing baseball with the likes of Harry Amato and Harvey Haddix. (*Don Rinker photo*)

acquisition is Harry Amato of Springfield, Ohio, a left-handed hitter and thrower who was this year's standout performer in the American Legion Junior Championships."

"Harry was known as a 'Bonus Baby,' and signed with Pittsburg during his junior year when he was 17," Don acknowledged. "The Springfield High School coaches were really upset that he wasn't able to play football during his senior year because he was quite a player, but the Pirates didn't want their rookie getting hurt.

"His family wasn't rich or poor but with the bonus money—which was $50,000 or $70,00 then—he bought his parents a new house," Don added.

During those early times, when a circus came to town, many of the animals arrived via train, Don recalled:

> We were living on Schaffer Street during the mid-1930s when the circus animals arrived in town into the Big Four Depot. The fairgrounds were where Davey Moore Park is today. They'd unload the circus animals at the depot and walk or wheel them in cages to the fairgrounds, up Pleasant Street. There was a big billboard on the corner of Western and Pleasant and all the kids used to climb up there to watch them walk in the animals. There were elephants, giraffes and zebras, as well as horses and camels. We'd watch them come in and sometimes the circus folks would let us help water the animals. The elephants walked trunk to tail and a lot of the animals—like lions and tigers—were in cages on wheeled wagons. Usually they came in and stayed for a couple of days. There were no fenced areas then so we could just kind of wander around and look at the animals.

When World War II broke out, it changed America forever. Don—fourteen years old at the time—was at the Majestic Theater watching a movie on Sunday, December 7, 1941, when it was interrupted by an announcement over the public address system. The Majestic, located at 23 South Limestone, had opened December 25, 1913 and was a 900-seat movie theater.

"I had gone there to see a Western movie," Don remembered:

> Back then, at the start of a show or afterward, there'd be a newsreel with updated news. After the first Western, a newsreel came on telling us the Japanese had bombed Pearl Harbor and that President Roosevelt was asking for a Declaration of War. I immediately left the theater and walked to the newspaper offices on Limestone and North, getting there just in time to catch a special edition they were printing. I grabbed 25 copies and headed back up towards the theater and by the time I got halfway back to the Majestic I'd sold all 25 copies, so I went back a second time and then a third time. With the third batch I walked toward home, down North Street and then Plum and when I got home, I had one paper left, which I gave to my mom, who was wondering why I was so late coming home from the movies.

During the summer months as a teenager, Don worked for the Coca-Cola bottling plant, located on North Street, not far from his Cedar Street digs.

Above: This photo shows the Big Top tent entrance to the Clyde Beatty and Cole Brothers Circus. (*Clark County Historical Society Archives)*

Below: Members of the combined Moores Brothers and Ringling Brothers Circus lead their ponies to the tents at the Springfield Fairgrounds in the 1940s. (*Clark County Historical Society Archives)*

Above: Elephants are led through the circus grounds in Springfield by staff members of the Moores Brothers and Ringling Brothers Circus. *(Clark County Historical Society Archives)*

Below: An elephant and his handler of the Moores Brothers and Ringling Brothers circus wait to perform in Springfield. *(Clark County Historical Society Archives)*

The Springfield Coca-Cola bottling plant, located in the 400 block of West North Street, where Don Rinker worked as a teenager. (*Clark County Historical Society Archives*)

"My sister Ruby worked there, and I got a delivery truck job when I was 14," Don stated:

> I had to take cases of Coke to the local grocery stores—two to three cases per week to each store. Each wooden case contained 24 bottles and you'd get paid two cents for the empty bottles you collected and one penny for the filled bottles that you delivered. I don't believe we got any kind of hourly wage beyond that.
>
> Jonathan Winters worked at the Coca Cola plant too. He worked on another truck because his friend's (Bill Collins') father (Holmes Collins) ran the plant. A lot of mornings when we would come in Winters would practice his radio show on us; he would do some of the characters like Ma Fricker that he did later in life. He was in high school then—we (all the helpers) would meet every morning—and the trucks would be loaded, and the drivers would be ready. You had to lift those cases off the truck, and they were heavy. They were stacked five cases up and about ten rows back and were angled so that they wouldn't fall off the truck as you drove it.

A truck delivers a shipment of Coca-Cola to the Silver Swan Inn and restaurant in 1941. The Silver Swan offered a batch of small cottages for weary travelers at the corner of Bird Road and Route 40 (Old National Road) and was often the home of visiting baseball teams who were in Springfield to battle the locals. Today, it is the site of a Marathon gas station and home to the Silver Swan Deli. *(Clark County Historical Society Archives)*

"That's where I learned to drive," he added. "My friend Harry Poulin, who was driving the truck regularly, pulled over on a hill one day and said, 'you're driving now.' It was a stick shift—there were no automatic trucks back then—and away we went, up and down the roads, stopping at all the little grocery stores on our route."

Don said, even then, Jonathon Winters had begun to make his presence felt: "He and Bill (Collins) and their buddies would go to the Van Cleve Hotel in Dayton on Saturday afternoons and apparently the hotel owners recognized Winters' talent because they let him perform, and then he and his group would eat and drink for free. They were all 18 or 19 then."

After attending Springfield High School during his sophomore and junior years, Don decided, along with friend Art Gueth, to enlist in the United States Coast Guard:

> There was a draft but if you enlisted you passed the draft, so Art (Gueth) and I joined the Coast Guard and they sent us to a Baltimore boot camp training us on landing craft, those that they drove into the Normandy beaches on D-Day. After basic training, they split us up and Art became a cook on a ship at Baltimore's Curtis Bay and I was sent on as a seaman on a ship called *Emporia Kansas*—a little ship about 300 feet long—and we cruised up and down the North Atlantic for the next two years.

Don Rinker (left) and Art Gueth (right) as U.S. Coast Guard sailors, 1944. (*Don Rinker photo*)

Don soon found himself in Reykjavik, Iceland, for three months, during the winter of 1944–45:

> Most people don't know this but there's a gulf stream of warm air that comes up from Florida in the winter months and it's fairly warm. When we were in Reykjavik it was our job to spot icebergs, enemy airplanes and submarines. We also sent up balloons that monitored the weather. Sometimes the seas were so rough that we wouldn't have survived if there hadn't been ropes tied all along the ship when we were out on the open ocean. We had to be especially careful at night when we were "on the watch" outside in the elements. We'd listen to WLW radio all night long when we were on duty, to a program called "*Moon River*" from the Cincinnati station. I was always amazed that we could get 700 WLW, even in Iceland. You could hear anybody from Rosemary Clooney to Fats Waller on there, and it made us quite nostalgic for home.

Back in Springfield, life was uncomplicated and unhurried, and local businesses thrived.

Above: Meek's Sporting Goods at its original location at 34 South Limestone Street sold everything from cameras to motorcycles, bicycles, hunting gear, outerwear, and toys such as Lionel Train sets. (*Clark County Historical Society Archives)*

Left: An ad from the *Springfield Daily News* in 1916 for Meek's Sporting Goods. (*Clark County Historical Society Archives)*

A more sophisticated ad in the *Springfield Daily News*, 1927, for Meek's Sporting Goods. (*Clark County Historical Society Archives)*

MEEK'S SPORTING GOODS

Meek's Sporting Goods was started in 1907 by George E. Meek and Charles T. Henderson, first located at 34 South Limestone Street. Incorporated in 1947 by George Meek (nephew of the founder), Henderson, and partner Ed Cozier, it was also the year Rinker became part of the local sporting goods store's team, which had moved its digs to 36–40 North Fountain Avenue.

"Meek's began as a bicycle and motorcycle shop and in the 1920s it evolved into a sporting goods store," Don stated:

> Ed Cozier got Meek's involved in the shotgun business and we became the largest dealer of clay targets in the country, because there were so many shooting clubs and big state shoots in the area such as the Grand American Handicap in Vandalia, and Meek's carried what everybody thought was a special kind of ammunition. We serviced all the local shooting clubs and used to deliver ammo in these big wooden cases which held 20 boxes.
>
> The ammo cost $25 a box, a good amount of money at the time. We also supplied all the local mom and pop stores in the area because back then, everybody sold ammo—places like Crabill's Hamburgers and the Catawba Market all sold ammo. Those wooden cases were heavy too, weighing in around 56–60 pounds.

After serving in the Coast Guard, Don had returned home to finish high school before playing baseball in the summer of 1947.

"I was playing ball and I didn't have a full-time job," Don said:

> Back then, when you came out of the service, they had a program called 52/20, that meant you got $20 for 52 weeks. It wasn't a lot of money, but it certainly helped. That September, Harry Amato told me that Meek's was looking for someone to write hunting licenses, so I applied and got the job. At that time, everyone who lived in the country purchased hunting licenses for $1.25 each and they'd be lined up out the door to get them. After the hunting season, Mr. Meek asked me to stay on to work the Christmas season.
>
> Meek's was very big at Christmas. We sold shotguns, rifles, fishing tackle, cameras, canoes, bicycles, trains and toys. The teams back then would buy a dozen baseballs and three bats—nothing like they do today. We'd deliver a lot of ammunition to the local shooting clubs too, like the Grand American Handicap and big trap shooting places in Mansfield and Indian Lake. I used to ride in the truck with Mr. Henderson and became good friends with him and George Meek—Mr. Meek's nephew. I was making $35 a week in then.

Alice Swisshelm had joined Meeks a few years earlier, after working for Ed Cozier's father at the Oliver Farm Equipment Company. She became not only Meek's longtime bookkeeper but was also adept at measuring bowling balls when Don was hired.

"You could hear George (Meek), because he whistled all the time," Alice related to Don. "But you rarely saw him. When you did, it was usually when he was repairing a bicycle, radio or motor of some type."

One of Don's first jobs was to dispose of Meek's trash at the local dump:

> We would take the trash there and it would catch fire from the hobos who were burning things to keep warm. A lot of the dumps at the time always had fires going. Meeks had a bunch of bowling balls that they wanted to throw away and at the time they were made of rubber, not plastic as they are today. We threw them in the fire, about 20 of them, and they caught and black smoke just started pouring out of them. The Springfield dump was located on old Dayton Avenue near the little league park. The guy who maintained the dump called George (Meek) and Eddie (Cozier) and told them never to throw bowling balls there again, as they created too much smoke and too much mess.

After the Christmas season, Rinker went on the road to play for a minor league baseball team, traveling throughout the East Coast during the spring of 1948. Don continued:

> There were a lot of minor teams and leagues then and I played for one out of Virginia. It was 'D' ball, which included teams like the Suffolk Goobers and the Springfield Giants. They sent me up to Delaware to play with a team out of Rehoboth Beach and I played throughout Virginia, North Caroline and Kentucky too. It was tough on the road. You didn't make a lot of money. They paid for your lunch and gave you a small amount to eat dinner on; about five bucks a day.

Above left: This ad from the *Springfield Daily News* in 1951 features a young Don Rinker (right) showing a customer the intricacies of a well-strung tennis racquet and how to properly grip a golf club. (*Don Rinker photo*)

Above right: The Buckeye Incubator Company's basketball team of 1950 included members Dave Stucky (standing, left), Ray Pfeiffer, Jim Hardman, and Bill Roth. Kneeling are George Winkhouse, Roland Delaney, and Don Rinker. Missing is teammate Blair Folck. Members of this District Championship team were the openers in the State AAU tournament in Dayton, Ohio. (*Don Rinker photo*)

> We always tried to save enough to grab a hot fudge sundae at night. We stayed in boarding houses and in the morning our breakfast was provided and at noon we got some sandwiches. Dinner was the meal money they gave us. About half-way through the season, Mr. Cozier called and asked if I wanted to work at Meek's full-time. Life on the road for a farm team player was not what it is today. We had a lot of tight quarters, not much money and were constantly traveling on a bus. I missed home and decided to go back. Working at Meeks sounded like a nice reprieve.

Rinker ended up working at Meeks for fifty-five years, eventually purchasing the company in 1976. Through the years, he learned every aspect of the sporting goods

The Springfield YMCA team was a formidable one in 1948, winning the state tournament that year against like-minded high schoolers. *Back row, left to right*: Paul Dunfee, unnamed, George Hennessey, Art Gueth, unnamed, and Tom Walsh. *Front row, left to right*: Bob Gueth, Don Rinker, Bud Cooper, Benny Martin, and Jim "Peachhead" Acton. (*Don Rinker photo*)

industry, and he also played on Springfield baseball and softball teams, as well as serving as a basketball and football referee throughout Ohio and surrounding states for more than four decades.

"In the 1950's, they'd send me on the road to purchase baseball bats," Don said:

> I'd take a truck and head to the Louisville Slugger factory in Louisville, Kentucky, and pick up 100 dozen wooden bats. They varied in price, with the top of the line bats costing $9. There was a Jackie Robinson bat, a Charlie Gerringer bat and they were all different based on weight, handle size. Often, they'd run out of the top line bats, so my boss Mr. Cozier told me to take a fifth of Jim Beam as an incentive to have them give me a few more dozen of their top bats. The company might tell me, we don't have any

Friends Art Gueth (left) and Don Rinker (right) hold up tickets to the 1950 State High School Basketball Tournament. The pair took turns standing in line from 7 p.m. the evening before the tickets went on sale at Springfield High School until the ticket office opened at 8 a.m. the next morning. After fourteen hours, they were able to purchase tickets to witness Springfield High School beat Akron South at the Ohio State Fairgrounds in Columbus, Ohio, one week later. (*Don Rinker photo*)

> more, and I'd pull out the bottle and I'd get a few more dozen of their top models. It's just the way things were done then.

Meek's also specialized in stretching baseball hats.

"Back then, baseball hats were all made of wool and it was cheap wool, usually," Don recalled. "We had a hat stretcher that made of a large piece of wood with a turning device in the center. When the hats got wet, they'd shrink, so a few turns on the hat stretcher would fix that."

The 1953 New Carlisle baseball team featured many talented Springfielders, including Don Rinker (second from left, top row); Frank Shannon (Ohio Wesleyan's head basketball coach & Wayne Embry's Tecumseh High School basketball coach); Dick Chaney (fourth from right); Flip Lucas (bottom left); George Winkhouse (fourth from left); and former Pittsburg Pirate pitcher Harry Amato (fourth from right). This team played won the state championship and traveled to Wichita, Kansas, to play a team from Casa Grande, Arizona, in the national championship. It was one of the first times that the national high school basketball championship was broadcast on radio. (*Don Rinker photo*)

Brooks Lawrence

Meeks had no shortage of local and national celebrities—both professional athletes and political figures—who visited the sporting goods store at 36 North Fountain Avenue.

"Davey Moore, who represented the 1952 Olympic boxing team, came into the store often," Don acknowledged:

> He had gone to Keifer Junior High School and didn't have a lot of money back then, but you could just tell he was a special individual.
>
> Brooks Lawrence was a very good football player at Springfield High School where I got to know him, and he always threw a baseball well. One day, in early 1954, Ed Cozier asked me, "Do you know where Brooks lives?" I said I did, and he said, "Go tell him he just got picked up by the St. Louis Cardinals." So, I went to Brooks' house over in the Sunnyland neighborhood on the south side, and he came to the door, and I said, "Eddie Cozier told me to congratulate you as you've been signed to play for the Cardinals." He said, "I can't imagine why, if you see the ball scores from yesterday, I got knocked out in the first inning!" He had no idea he was going to the Major Leagues,

> but he did come into Meek's in later years to order his special Riddell shoes with toe plates on them.

Born in Springfield on January 30, 1925, Brooks Ulysses Lawrence was the fifth of six children of Wilbur Lawrence and Patsie Walker Lawrence. He would later become a Major League Baseball All-Star pitcher for the St. Louis Cardinals (1954–1955) and the Cincinnati Reds (1956–1960). His father had been a sharecropper in Sparta, Georgia, and had moved the family to Springfield in 1922. Early on, Brooks showed a passion for the game of baseball. As a seventh grader, he tried out on the Springfield sandlots—acquiring a spot on the Pump House Gang roster. At Kiefer Junior High School, Brooks played on both the basketball and track teams, and in the ninth grade, he led the football team to an undefeated season and city championship.

During his first year at Springfield High School, his gridiron abilities should have escalated him to a position as starting quarter, but racial prejudices forbade having a black quarterback. Finally, in his 1941–1942 school year (junior), he made history as the school's first black starting quarterback, leading the Wildcats to a winning season (their first in ten years), while serving as the basketball team's forward for their Greater Ohio Basketball Championship winning title. He then went on to serve on the track team, which captured the district title and finished second in the state. That year, he won letters in football, basketball, and track.

Baseball was a segregated sport at Springfield High School in those days until Brooks got a group together who opposed the white team, beating them by a 15:2 score. Baseball Coach Russ Paugh agreed to use Brooks for the Championship, but it never came to fruition, as the team failed to qualify. After graduating in 1943, Lawrence served in World War II in Guam in a segregated Army Engineers unit; he returned in December 1945 with a Bronze Star emblazoned on his chest.

After attending Miami University of Ohio in 1947 for two years, Brooks alternated his field time between his college team and the Springfield Tigers, and he played in the Negro National League. A tryout for the Dayton Indians (Cleveland's Class A farm team) got him signed, and he was called up by the Cardinals on June 24, 1954, where he pitched his career debut with a 5:1 victory over the Pittsburg Pirates at Forbes Field at the age of twenty-nine. He then pitched six more consecutive wins, ending his first season with a 15:6 record in the majors.

Brooks was traded midway through his 1956 season to Cincinnati, winning thirteen games before suffering his first lost. He was named to the National League All-Star team that year—where eight Reds served—but did not pitch in the game and wrapped up the season with a 19:10 record. Known to recite poetry and other literary works, Lawrence's pitching career in 1960 after 275 games, saw a record of 69:62, and a career ERA of 4.25.

"Back then, the players had to buy their own shoes, and guys like Brooks and Harvey Haddix would always buy them from Meek's," Don explained. "They needed those toe plates on the shoes to help them withstand the wear and tear when the pitcher dragged his toe. Brooks later became in charge of ticket sales for the Reds during the winter months."

Lawrence lived out his days working for Springfield-based International Harvester and later in customer sales, radio broadcast, and scouting for the Reds. He coached

Above left: Springfield native Brooks Lawrence was a star athlete at Springfield High School before being drafted into the Major Leagues baseball ranks. (*Don Rinker photo*)

Above right: Official Cincinnati Reds photo of Brooks Lawrence in 1956. (*Don Rinker photo*)

Wilmington College's baseball team from 1988 to 1993, where his team garnered a 97:91 record and won a pair of Midwest College Championships. Brooks was recognized as 1992 AMC Coach of the Year, and prior to his death on April 27, 2000, he worked with the Baseball Assistance Team (BAT—an organization to help in-need, older players) and was named to the Springfield South High School Hall of Fame, the Ohio Baseball Hall of Fame, the Cincinnati Reds Hall of Fame, and the Wilmington College Athletic Hall of Fame.

William Saxbe

William Saxbe was a Mechanicsburg-based attorney and former Ohio Attorney General (1963–1969) and Ohio State Senator (1969–1974) who would also frequent Meek's on occasion.

"Bill Saxbe came into the store quite often," Don said:

> Once, we had to measure him for a gun that Winchester was presenting to him during an appearance on the Ed Sullivan Show. He had a place up in Mechanicsburg called the Van Dyke Club and they'd have trap shoots there and invite folks like Jack Nicolas, businessmen and Ohio politicians. They'd have a big, all-game dinner for the guys. I'd go up and set up the traps of clay birds that they shot out over the lake. Bill was really a nice person and well-liked.

Saxbe later became President Richard Nixon's fourth attorney general, taking office in 1974. He resigned on February 1, 1975 under President Gerald Ford to become ambassador to India, a post he held until November 20, 1975. He eventually returned to Mechanicsburg, resuming his law practice.

SPARROW YOUNG

"Sparrow Young used to come into the store," Don noted. "He shot the first ever 100-straight from 23 yards at the 1926 Grand American Handicap in Vandalia. He used to tell us stories about his friend Annie Oakley, who was from Greenville, Ohio."

Charles "Sparrow" Young was one of the nation's most talented trap shooters in the United States in the 1920s, and he had originally broken the 25-straight record at the first Grand American Handicap in 1900 in New York City under the moniker of Robin Hood. He broke 100-straight from 23 yards at Peru, Indiana, in 1916 before setting the record in 1926. His nickname came from the late 1800s when live sparrows were used instead of clay targets. Young won numerous live and pigeon professional and

Charles "Sparrow" Young, shown here at a Springfield shoot in 1927. (*Don Rinker photo*)

amateur events, winning the 1893 Chicago World's Fair Trapshooting Championship. He became a gunsmith, inventing the release trigger, among his other talents. He was also a professional shooter for Remington. Don recalls many a trip he took with Charles:

> Charlie was a neat old character and when I'd go deliver ammunition, say to DeGraff or Russell's Point, he'd ride along. Once, we went up to DeGraff Gun Club and ordered lunch at a small diner. We ate, then Charlie picked up the check and took it out to the truck and said, "let's go." At Meek's he used to sit by the old coke machine where there was a bat rack. Charlie would always peek around the rack to see who was coming through the back door. He rode the bus every day and we had a big green chair in the gun department at Meeks' that he'd sit in, too. Charlie would go into Gallaher's drug store on the southeast corner of Fountain and Main every day, where the City Building is today, and have lunch. One day he came back and said, "I'm not feeling well, could you take me home." I drove him to his home on Huron Avenue and he died that night.

Sparrow Young passed away quietly on May 15, 1951 at the age of eighty-five.

Will McEnaney

Major league pitcher Will McEnaney—who was featured on the November 3, 1975 cover of *Sports Illustrated* jumping into the arms of catcher Johnny Bench after the Cincinnati Reds captured the World Series—was a Springfield native and another Meek's regular.

"Will McEnaney and his brother Mike were a pair of crazy twins who were great athletes," Don recalled. "When they'd play baseball in high school, their coach Don Henderson told me they'd switch uniforms just to mess with people. They were funny and wild, and very popular."

McEnaney was a left-handed pitcher who played with the Cincinnati Reds, Montreal Expos, Pittsburg Pirates, and St. Louis Cardinals from 1974–1979. Born on February 14, 1952, McEnaney was one of five children raised by William and Eleanor Grieb McEnaney. After graduating from Springfield North High School, he was nabbed by the Reds in the eighth round in 1970 amateur draft and made his Major League debut four years later on July 3, 1974 at Riverfront Stadium. He relieved pitcher Clay "Hawk" Carroll, pitching to the Los Angeles Dodgers, in a 4:1 loss. His first inning saw him score pop outs from Tommy John, Davey Lopez, and Bill Buckner, and he did pitch two scoreless innings despite the loss in his debut.

As a rookie, he pitched in twenty-four games, with a 2:1 record and 4.44 ERA. McEnaney was a manager's dream for the next two seasons—during the heyday of the "Big Red Machine" in which the Reds were the 1975 and 1976 World Champions. In 1975, he scored fifteen saves in seventy pitching appearances with a 5:2 record and 2.47 ERA and pitched 6.2 innings in five of the World Series games, with a 2.70 ERA and one save. He pitched the final inning of that year's decisive World Series game, as the Reds were leading 4:3 over the Boston Reds Sox, enticing Juan Beniquez to fly out,

Above left: Springfield native Will McEnaney became a celebrated pitcher for the Cincinnati Reds in the mid-1970s. (*Don Rinker photo*)

Above right: The cover of *Sports Illustrated* from November 3, 1975 featured a celebratory embrace between Cincinnati Reds pitcher Will McEnaney and catcher Johnny Bench after the Reds won the World Series. (*Author photo*)

Bob Montgomery to groundout, and Carl Yastrzemski to fly out. The photograph of he and catcher Johnny Bench embracing on the pitcher's mound on the cover of *Sports Illustrated* that year remains a classic.

The following season saw McEnaney pitch in fifty-five games with a 2:6 record and 4.85 ERA, but once again, he excelled in the World Series, pitching 4.2 scoreless innings and securing two saves. For the second straight year, he pitched a 1:2:3 ninth inning to retire the New York Yankees in a four-game sweep for the 1976 World Series crown. Despite his brilliance, McEnaney was traded to the Expos in December of that year and then to the Pirates for the 1978 season, before playing for the Cardinals in 1979. He retired from the Majors in 1908 with a 12:17 record and 3.76 ERA, with 148 strikeouts in 269 times on the mound as a reliever. He currently resides in Florida.

The Meek's storefront in 1958, now located at 36–40 North Fountain Avenue. (*Clark County Historical Society Archives)*

Later Years

In the 1970s, 1980s, and 1990s, Meek's expanded, opening stores at Springfield's Upper Valley Mall and in nearby Wilmington and Piqua, and for a short while, it was the only Nike dealer around. But the original downtown location remained a hotspot where coaches and athletes congregated, especially on Saturday afternoons. Meek's Christmas Eve parties were legendary.

"The relationships we forged with the coaches, the school folks, and the kids were the things that make a town like Springfield work," Alice recalled. "Those relationships aren't sprung overnight."

Saturday afternoons found poker games in one of Meek's three basements. Don once staged a fake police raid as a joke on coach Danny Winters whose father-in-law was a judge. "Mike Peters, a local cop knew most of the guys who frequented the poker game," Don noted:

> The coaches were in the basement playing poker when a paddy wagon backed up to the loading ramp in the parking lot. Cops came running in and coaches went scattering. Some were hiding in corners of the basements and some ran upstairs and hid in my office and Alice's office. It took a while before everyone realized it was a prank.

And those Christmas Eves at Meek's were not without drama either. "Once, just prior to closing time, a lady who was half-drunk came in wanting to buy a sled and bicycle," Don laughed:

> And to top it off, she wanted them delivered. Now here it is, 5:30 on Christmas Eve and it's snowing to beat the band. We had a kid named Jimmy Waters, who was a Wittenberg student, working for us and he agrees to deliver her stuff, but all he has is a convertible. So, he pulls his car up, puts the top down and it's still snowing, loads up her items, and drives off. Those are the kinds of wacky things that happen when you run a business.[1]

8

Nothing Short of Lagonda

James Lough, eighty-five years old in 2020 and a lifelong Springfielder, has fond memories of what life was like growing up in Springfield's Lagonda neighborhood during the mid-twentieth century.

"If you weren't raised in the Lagonda neighborhood, you were shortchanged," he mused. "We were dirt poor and didn't have material things, but we had the neighborhood, sports, the local swimming pool and each other. We thought we owned the world back then."

Born on August 30, 1935 at home on Summit Avenue and known to everyone as "Jimmie," the son of Preston and Minnie Lough was one of twelve children and grew up on Edwards Avenue during the 1930s and 1940s.

"We used to spend a lot of our summer days at Roger's Beach on Belmont," Jimmie recalled. "It was in the parking lot of the old International Harvester, across from Lucky Lanes Bowling Alley. Johnson's Box Lunch—a local eatery—served everybody in the area with fantastic food."

> There was a horse stables there too, on the corner of Mitchell Blvd across from Karanos Root Beer Stand. You could ride horses there for 25 cents for 15 minutes. A lady named Mary with a wooden leg ran the place, and we kids would take the horses out way longer than we were supposed to, because we knew there wasn't anything Mary could do to stop us. Softball was big back then too. The playgrounds were always full and back then, parents acted as supervisors at these spots. One parent who'd watch us was named Theodore Felton Young, who everybody called "Bob," and he'd talk about "riding the rails," saying how he'd jump onto a train and tie himself to the roof with his belt to go back and forth between cities when he needed to.

In later years, "cruising was the thing for high school kids to do," Jimmie laughed. "We'd drive to various drive-in restaurants, looking for girls. We had a lot of fun back then."

When he was aged thirteen, Jimmie took a job as a pinsetter at Lagonda Lanes bowling alley, a profession shared by his longtime friend Don Rinker.

"They only had four lanes and we each worked two lanes at a time," Jimmie recalled.

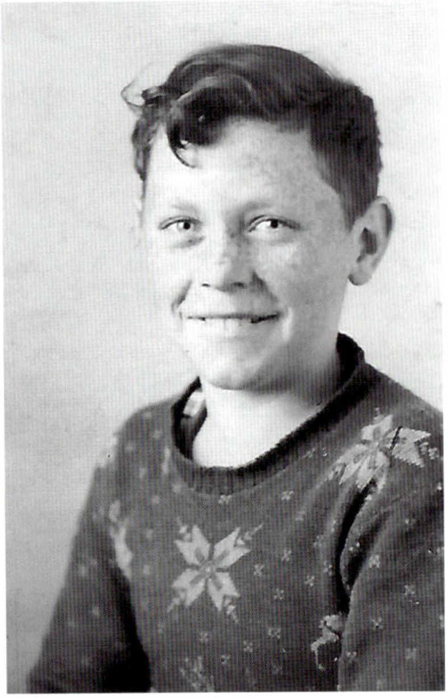

Left: Jimmie Lough, aged eight, in his third grade photo. (*James Lough photo*)

Below: Rogers Beach in Springfield was a public pool where local kids like Jimmie Lough could go to swim and socialize. (*Clark County Historical Society Archives)*

Above: One of Springfield's largest industrial manufacturers was International Harvester, shown in here in a photo from 1934. (*Clark County Historical Society Archives)*

Right: Jimmie Lough, in his baseball uniform for the Springfield American Legion Post, stands beside his mother, Minnie, at their house on Edwards Avenue in the Lagonda neighborhood. (*James Lough photo*)

Jimmie Lough steers his pacer to victory at his home track of the Urbana Fairgrounds in 1977. Besides playing on numerous local baseball and softball teams, Jimmie was an active trainer-driver of harness horses in his younger years and still works in the barn as of this writing, assisting in the training of the family's race horses. (*James Lough photo*)

"The pay was about $1.50 an hour."

With the money he earned, Jimmie would go to minstrel and vaudeville performances at Memorial Hall. In his late teens and early twenties, he was a sub for the Springfield Giants baseball team and played on many softball teams, including the local Pabst team.

The Social Scene

Jimmie and his wife, Lindy, were no strangers to the Springfield social scene, often frequenting such spots as the Cabanas Club at 3484 Valley Pike. Located inside the Lakewood Swim & Athletic Club, the Cabanas Club—later renamed the Coconut Lounge—seated up to 500 people and was where Springfielders came to party and see acts of the 1950s and 1960s, Lindy, Jimmie's wife of fifty-nine years, recalled.

"We saw a lot of top acts there," Lindy noted.

> Groups like the Four Seasons, The Kingsmen, Jan and Dean and the Beach Boys played there. It wasn't tough to get a good, reliable babysitter in those days, either. You could call up Community Hospital if you wanted to go out. They had nurses in training and they offered babysitting services and didn't charge a lot. That was an option a lot of

The American Restaurant, located on Washington and Limestone Streets, was a Springfield favorite among high school students and adults alike in the 1950s. (*Clark County Historical Society Archives*)

The Crystal Restaurant, a high-end restaurant located downtown, was co-owned by Nick and Gus Panos and their cousin, Gus Mantis. The Panos brothers immigrated to Springfield from Greece around 1912. (*Clark County Historical Society Archives*)

us used in those days.

A self-proclaimed "food enthusiast," Jimmie has no problem remembering some of his favorite Springfield hangouts from that era.

"In the early 1950s, you could get a great meal at the American Restaurant, on the corner of Limestone and Washington Streets," Jimmie stressed. "It cost 55 cents for a plate of spaghetti and it was delicious. Gus Keriosis ran it and it was a popular spot among the high school kids."

"There was the Elite Restaurant, a great steak house located at Wittenberg and Main streets across from the Crowell-Collier plant," he recalled. "Then Jim's, near the Regent Theater, who made great olive and ham sandwiches—nobody made olive sandwiches like Jim's."

"You had Webbs, a great hamburger joint on Main Street and the Top Hat, on East Main," Jimmie added. "Another great place for burgers was Scotty's and one of the best ice cream shops was Kohl's Dairy on Clairmont Avenue near Warder Park."

"Movies were always a great option too," Jimmie admitted. "Besides the Regent, the Princess, Majestic and State theaters, we had the Hippodrome, The Fairbanks and Liberty. Springfield really had a lot of options in those days for young people. We always had a place to go for a great meal and for not a lot of money, either."[1]

Jimmie and Linda Lough. (*James Lough photo*)

9

One of Springfield's Finest

Thor Ronemus was born on November 27, 1930 in Springfield to Louis Gladden and Irene Massie Ronemus. Thor's great-grandfather immigrated to the United States from Germany, dropping the "Hi" from the family name (Hironemus) and settling in South Charleston.

"He was a tailor," recalled Kyle Ronemus, Thor's youngest son (aged fifty-nine) who resides in California. "Dad's father—who everyone called Ronnie—was quite a character. He was principal and the athletic director and track and cross-country coach at South High School. He became a county commissioner for many years and was a starter for the canoe races at Mad River I attended as a youngster. His wife Irene was the classic old school housewife."

Kyle, along with his brothers, Eric (aged sixty-five), Mike (aged sixty-four), and Andy (aged sixty-one), would regularly accompany their father in his canoeing excursions.

"We went all over Indiana, Michigan, Illinois and Ohio," Kyle stated. "Dad lived to paddle and did canoeing right up until the end."

Prior to raising his family with Springfield High School sweetheart Nancy Baylor Ronemus, Thor had been an outstanding athlete and was selected to the first string 1947 All-Ohio Football Team, serving as captain in 1948.

Thor exceled in sports at The Ohio State University, where he served under coaches Wes Fesler and Woody Hayes, while pursuing his Bachelor of Science in business administration and Juris Doctor law degrees. Thor was the Buckeye's right guard from 1949 through 1951. Kyle said:

> Dad played for Woody the first year he was coaching at OSU. He always said that Woody was way more volatile in those early years. Once, dad got hurt during the first half of a game. In those days, if you got hurt, you left the field, went to the locker room and then into the stands. Dad went into the stands to sit with his parents and watch the rest of the game and had the locker room key in his pocket. Unbeknownst to Dad, he had forgotten to leave the locker room door unlocked. Woody was so furious that he couldn't get in the locker room that he ripped the door off the hinges. When Dad went back after the game, a friend told him he better not run into Woody as the coach was furious over the missing key.

Left: Thor Ronemus' Springfield High School portrait. (*Don Rinker photo*)

Below: Thor with high school sweetheart and wife of twenty-nine years, Nancy Baylor Ronemus. (*Kyle Ronemus photo*)

> Dad knew the great quarterback and Heisman Trophy winner Howard "Hopalong" Cassidy and a lot of the great players. He used to take us to the Ohio State locker room at Ohio Stadium when we were kids and I'd see all these famous guys—like Archie Griffin—running around in towels.

Thor was a member of the Sigma Chi Fraternity and a Mason, and he famously participated in the "Snow Bowl" on November 25, 1950 in Ohio Stadium in Columbus. The game for the Big Ten Conference Championship pitted Ohio State against fierce rival Michigan. Some 50,535 fans attended that day, building fires in the stands to keep warm during the blizzard that ensued.

"Dad said that nobody could move the ball that day," Kyle stressed. "My mom and grandparents sat through that game in the freezing cold. It was like ten degrees with 30 mile per hour winds and the snow never stopped. Dad said they could hardly see the goal posts."

Despite getting three first downs and punting twenty-one times, the Buckeyes lost to the Wolverines—who punted twenty-four times without garnering a first down or completing a pass—9:3, giving Michigan their fourth straight title and ending Fesler's career. He was replaced by Woody Hayes two weeks later.

Thor practiced law for fifty-three years in Ohio and Florida, and he kept his ties with his *alma mater* close, serving as president of Ohio State's Varsity "O" Club. He was president of the Clark County Bar Association, a Springfield University Club officer, and member of the Springfield City Civil Service Commission, Ohio State Bar Association, Ohio State Alumni Association, and Springfield Polo Club.

"Dad was very active in Springfield," Mike Ronemus, a Connecticut-based attorney, said. "He loved the town and all of the characters. He used to go to Jim's coffee shop every day for lunch because he said they had the best olive sandwiches."

But it was canoeing that Thor Ronemus held most dear, serving as a 1968 charter member and vice-president of the United States Canoe Association and Ohio delegate until his death on January 3, 2009.

"Dad just loved canoeing," Kyle stressed. "He won the national USCA Canoe Championship in 1969 and 1970 and would go down the rivers on his one-person cedar strip. It was his passion."

"We all raced canoes because of dad," Mike Ronemus confirmed.

> Dad was so supportive of whatever sport we did—he loved the fact that we all played high school football and always came to watch us and brought our grandfather along. Dad was a very smart guy who was proud of anyone in the family that did anything scholarly. He was very encouraging and loved doing things with family. We were skiing together in Montana only a few months before he died of a heart attack. He was the type of guy that just really enjoyed life.[1]

Thor Ronemus in his gridiron outfit as a starter for the Ohio State Buckeyes. (*Don Rinker photo*)

The Ronemus Family: Thor and Nancy holding son, Kyle. Seated are sons Andy, Mike, and Eric. (*Kyle Ronemus photo*)

10

The Heaume Hotel & Jacamar Tea Room

Nancy Baylor Ronemus, Thor's wife of twenty-nine years and lifelong friend, came from a Springfield family with deep ties to Clark County. Nancy's maternal grandparents (John "Jack" Sallady and Julia Heaume) built the Heaume Hotel, located on the southeast corner of Fountain Avenue and Columbia Street, after purchasing the property from the Masonic Lodge in 1914.

The couple opened the "Interurban Lunch & Dining Hall" across the street from where the Heaume Hotel would eventually stand, and in 1915, they began construction on their vision.

"John's first small restaurant—The Interurban—was so named because it connected with the Interurban ticket office," Julia Heaume wrote in her memoirs. "It was a small, two-room restaurant on North Fountain. Mama helped a lot and John's restaurant prospered. Mama's stewed chicken and biscuits (was) a leader."

"John paid $23,500 for this house and lot and moved into it after adding to the front of the old house," Julia continued. "For about five years, he ran the restaurant and rented out the bedrooms upstairs."

"Jack built the hotel there because that's where the train tracks stopped coming in from the East," Kyle said. "It became one of the best hotels and restaurants in Ohio."

"Father Heaume owned 29 feet adjoining this building and gave this to John, who sold half of it and added to what he had saved, started planning the (present) hotel building," Julia wrote. "The architect and builder, George Ohmart, was engaged and soon the old frame was razed, and work begun on the new hotel."

"During the building period, John rented a room just north of the alley behind Wren's store and continued his restaurant business there," Julia continued:

> During the hotel construction, a strike was called by some Union workers. They stood outside John's restaurant passing out cards reading 'Don't patronize this restaurant. His hotel is being built unfair to labor.' Naturally this increased John's business. All cards were placed in a box at the (Interurban's) cashier's desk. When the box was filled, the cards were taken out to the men passing them. They were told to keep on giving these out as it was greatly helping our business. Then soon the strike collapsed.

Right: Nancy Baylor's Springfield High School portrait. Her maternal grandparents, Jack and Julia Heaume, built Springfield's famed Heaume Hotel. (*Don Rinker photo*)

Below: The Interurban Restaurant, located at 31 South Fountain Avenue, was so named because it connected with the interurban ticket office. Founded and owned by John and Julie Heaume, it opened in 1909 with great success. This same couple then opened the Heaume Hotel in 1917, directly across the street at the corner of Fountain and Columbia Streets. (*Clark County Historical Society Archives*)

Interurban lines once crisscrossed throughout Springfield as this photo at the Big Four Depot in the late 1900s shows. In the first decade of the twentieth century, the interurban line of electric trolleys—also known as traction cars—were established to move citizens from town to town. By 1905, Springfield was able to move horses on the interurban cars with passengers using the front baggage compartments. The regular luxury trolleys featured electric fans in the main compartment with electric cigar lighters in the men's room and curling irons in the ladies' room. Some of the interurban cars could travel as fast as 80 miles per hour on a straight route. The 45-ton cars were powered by four, 150-horsepower motors through overhead, electrical wires. The advent of the interurbans truly bridged the gap between the horse and buggy and automobile eras, with the earliest interurbans utilized in the Sandusky, Ohio, region. The word "interurban" is derived from the Latin phrase meaning "between cities." By the mid-1930s—as more and more folks purchased their own automobiles—the interurbans were down to just three major lines in Springfield. The Snyder Park, Limestone, and Lagonda were all that remained until they finally shut down on October 29, 1938 as the last of the Cincinnati and Lake Erie cars rambled through Springfield. (*Clark County Historical Society Archives)*

Opposite: The ad for a new Charlie Chaplin film *Police* at Springfield's Princess Theater appeared in the *Springfield Daily News* in the June 13, 1916 edition, while the Heaume Hotel was still under construction. The timetable for the Big Four Depot schedule is located directly below. (*Clark County Historical Society Archives)*

PRINCESS

TODAY AND TOMORROW

Charlie Chaplin

In His Latest Comedy.

"Police"

A screaming Button-Ripper—2000 feet of laughs—Rip-Roaring laughs.

FIRST TIME HERE

Also showing "John Brewsters Wife," Mutual Masterpiece.

COMING THURSDAY AND FRIDAY

J. J. Corbett

Famous Prize Fighter in "THE BURGLAR AND THE LADY"

Through Sleeping Car Service to

Indianapolis and Chicago

Big Four Route

Car may be occupied at Indianapolis until 7:00 a. m.

TICKETS AT SPRINGFIELD DEPOT TICKET OFFICE

E. B. GORSUCH, Gen'l Agt. Pass. Dept.

Lv. Springfield	10:45 pm.
Ar. Indianapolis	2:00 am.
Ar. Chicago	7:20 am.

Telephones: Home Main 49 Bell Main 991 and 992

The five-story, fireproof Heaume Hotel opened for business on August 31, 1917 with eighty rooms and featured the Jacamar Tea Room; the name a combination of the Heaume's three children: Jack, Jr., Catherine, and Marjorie. The Heaume boasted rates of $1.50 and up for a single room and $8 and up for a double room. Every room had a private bath and was first class in both style and amenities, with custom sculpted wood furniture, a modern elevator, and ornate lobby.

"Flowers, plants and good wishes, plus more people in the Jacamar than we could handle," Julia wrote:

> Of course, the new stove in the kitchen slowed down and some (patrons) had slow service. I was working as a cashier in the northwest corner when someone paraded to the desk and said, "You will have to give better service than this or else you will fail." I was dead-tired anyway and tears rolled down my cheeks. I can't forget Elbe Brubaker coming up then to pay his check and saying, "Cheer up—the idea of crying over too much business!" That day I worked wherever needed—even ran the elevator when the boy was out for lunch.

"So, life began for John as a hotel man," Julia continued:

> J. M Brust of the C.D. Kenny Coffee Company was the first to register as a guest. At that time our slogan was 'A room with a bath for a dollar and a half' and so it was for years. The same room now rents for $3.00 to $3.50. Business was very good, as it had to be for John to meet his many notes, plus bank interest. Residents patronized our food department and a 'full house' was the general condition then. Incidents of the hotel could fill a book!

Julia recounted many interesting tales in her writings, some humorous and some not:

> An old couple taken to their room had never before been in a hotel. Said the bell hop to them: "When you want anything, just phone the clerk." Soon a call came: "We are ready to come down. What do we do now?" Clerk: "Just ring elevator bell."
>
> Once Ted Pruitt saw water coming under the doorway into a hall, entered, found the bathroom door closed and water pouring out into the room. The naked man inside said, "I was waiting for the water to reach my knees, but it never got over my feet."
>
> One drunk set his bed afire; smoke brought every occupant out into the hallway. Soon the drunk appeared demanding John pay for burns on his hands. John's reply is unprintable. Nancy, a little girl then, explained to an old fellow who appeared in long red underwear, "Some man with a disease set fire to his bed." Said man had a cleft palate.

"One suicide affected me greatly," Julia wrote:

> A nicely-dressed man registered in from Dayton. Soon a shot was heard from his room. On his dresser were his underclothes neatly folded, on the floor of the bathroom, he had placed a towel, then sat on it and shot himself. He was, even in this awful moment, thoughtful enough not to have our room blood-stained. Discovered later that he was having marital troubles.

An August 1917 ad for the Westcott Six, the newest automobile by the Westcott Motor Car Company of Springfield, established in 1916 in Clark County. Known as one of the Westcott Touring Cars, it was elegance personified. The hand-assembled vehicle was built at the Warder Street plant and featured a six-cylinder engine along with its four-door sedan design. Burton J. Westcott, born in Richmond, Indiana, in 1868, was one of Springfield's most prominent and successful businessmen who came to Springfield in 1903 to oversee his father's (John M. Westcott) American Seeding Machine Company, located on the southwest corner of Liberty Avenue and Plum Street. Burton Westcott was a member of the Springfield Town Council from 1916 to 1922, a Lagonda National Bank director and Springfield Country Club member until his death on January 10, 1926. His home at 1340 East High Street was designed by Frank Lloyd Wright in 1908 and is the only prairie-style house designed by the architect in Ohio. Purchased by the Frank Lloyd Wright Building Conservancy of Chicago in 2000, it was sold to Springfield's Westcott House Foundation and underwent a $5.3 million restoration that took five years to complete. It opened in October 2005 to guided public tours. (*Clark County Historical Society Archives)*

The Heaume Hotel in 1935 on the corner of North Fountain Avenue. The three buildings next to it at 36, 38, and 40 North Fountain Avenue would later become the home of Meek's Sporting Goods. *(Clark County Historical Society Archives)*

> Another girl was not so thoughtful—broke a glass, lay across the bed and cut her wrists. She was discovered and taken to a hospital. So, life went on as of course it has to in other hotels.

Prior to the Great Depression, the Heaume children all attended Northern School, then Springfield High School on South Limestone. After graduation, Marjorie (Nancy Ronemus' mother) went to Painesville School for Girls; Catherine to Gibbons in Boston; and Jack to Wittenberg, Cornell, and The Ohio State University.

"Soon the big Depression hit us hard," Julia wrote:

> Jack was at Cornell and he had to be called home. We lost our home at 1601 Woodedge and moved into 504, 505 and 506 at the hotel. Being on the top floor, I didn't always pull down the blind until one day Chef Edgewood said to John "the men at the Metallic Casket company are having a lot of fun watching some woman on the fifth-floor bathe." These men were using telescopes of course, to watch me bathe!

"How we lived through the Depression, I'll never know," she continued:

> We did manage to rent 1601 Woodedge and finally sell it at a loss, but had enough from it to send Jack to O.S.U. We found we had so many loyal friends in those days. Had it not been for Billy Mills of the M and M Bank, Bill Trout of Bordan's Milk Company; and our good advisor and friend Stewart Tatum, we would never have

Springfield Metallic Casket Company advertisement from 1913. (*Clark County Historical Society Archives)*

> survived. Frank Krapp, and what a villain he turned out to be, pushed for a foreclosure, even offering Pearl Crabill the hotel at our indebtedness to M and M. She told him, "No, I won't treat Johnny that way." Somehow, we pulled through, but we shall never forget the friends who stood by us those awful days.

"After the Depression, people started driving their own cars everywhere, and the train lines were removed," Kyle Ronemus explained. "Hotels became motels. So old school hotels like the Heaume had it tough. Jack worked with a local banker and was able to save the hotel through the Depression and later Marjorie (Nancy's mom & the Ronemus boys' maternal grandmother) took it over."

"After the Depression was over, things became easier for us," Julia wrote: "Our mortgage on the hotel was cancelled and business prospered, and we paid off all mortgages in 1952. Then came the Motels and we've not made money, but still hope to survive. John semi-retired when he was 75 but still retained control and ownership."

"We now have a fine manager, Bruce Thompson, who also runs the Hangar Bar," Julia penned after the Great Depression:

A match cover from the Heaume Hotel's Jacamar Tea Room. (*Don Rinker photo*)

> For some reason, John has no scruples against a bar, but refuses to have it called by his name. The Jacamar Tea room was the best spot for good food in Springfield. One "big table" in each room had our finest businessmen each noon: Frank Dock, Reese Tulloss, Harry Bretnay, Chase Stewart, Dr. Howell, Frank Mills, George Winwood, Horace Keifer, Dr. Hullinger, C.M. Beckett, Bob Hawken, John Jessee, Bob Rewey, Bill Trout, Dr. Elliott, John Fox, Howell Jones, and Bob Ramsey.
>
> I recall Elba Brubaker used to phone from the hospital to have a pot of double strength coffee ready for him. He reeked of either; and Harry Freeman phoned to have ready a bowl of French onion soup—topped by toast and cheese. I recall little Chase Stewart leaving the lobby one day with a very tall man's overcoat dragging on the floor. Bill McCulloch (was) always at the end of the counter and mixing mashed potatoes and sauerkraut.

The Jacamar Tea Room was especially noted for its salad bowl and homemade pies.

> We had two fine chefs—Edgewood and Mike Cledis. Pastry cooks—Alex Thomas and sister Margaret who is pastry girl at our Country Club, and Maude and Goldie, our salad girls.
>
> The men's big table was a wild bunch—Frank Dock loved to call John back to see a crack in a cup, then drop it to the floor, much to John's dismay, but probably justified. When Wright-Patterson Field paid double (to employees) what we could, many of our food employees left for there, so the old and famous Jacamar closed.

"When Marjorie took over, she closed the restaurant and ran the Hangar Bar (located in between the Heaume & Meeks) and it became a pretty wild place," Kyle recalled. "Marjorie

The Myers Market Building in 1926 was a quick walk from the Heaume Hotel. (*Clark County Historical Society Archives)*

was a classic flapper girl right out of the 1920s. The doorman was a character too, his name was Harvel and he'd escort patrons up to their floors via that old-fashioned elevator."

"Everybody in town knew Harvel," Jimmie Lough acknowledged. "He was very well-liked and always impeccably dressed. You knew if went to the Heaume for a drink or a sandwich, that Harvel would be there to greet you."

Harvel—an African American gentleman whose last name remains a mystery—was one of Springfield's first openly gay persons of color. "Harvel was so sweet to us and always made sure we had a good time," Mike Ronemus remembered:

> We'd go to the hotel and play with the switchboard and go up and down the elevator and have a blast. The elevator was one of the old-fashioned kinds with a sliding metal gate and it had a handle you could move back and forth to make it go up and down. After we got tired of that we'd go next door to Meek's (Sporting Goods) to look around at all the cool stuff and then head back to the bar that was in between the Heaume and Meek's. We'd go in there with our grandma (Marjorie). She had a shooting range in there and a standup shuffleboard game. There were a lot of folks in there on Sundays pounding drinks, too.

"The Hangar Bar was a lot of fun for the locals," recalled Don Rinker. "They used to have one of those ticker-tape machines in there, a variant of the wire machines used by newspapers, and we'd go in there to get the results of the baseball games as they came over the wire."

The Heaume Hotel remained open for fifty-six years, eventually closing its doors on October 5, 1973.[1]

11

The Mayor of Main Street

James William "Jim" Lopez, known to many in Springfield as "The Mayor of Main Street," had the distinction of opening the first Taco Bell east of the Mississippi in Springfield in 1968.

Lopez's family had immigrated to the United States from Castelvetriano, a village on Sicily's southwestern corner, with the name being shortened from Lopezini to Lopez.

"My grandfather was born William Lopezini and he came to the United States through Ellis Island when he was eight-years-old," Jimmy Lopez, James's son, said. "He was born in Sicily in 1900 and died in 1996. He lived a real simple life."

Jimmy, who runs Big Jim's on Bechtle Avenue, fondly remembers his grandfather who worked for Pittsburg's Plate Glass Company.

"He never ate any fried food, he boiled everything and always had a garden, no matter where he lived," Jimmy said. "His wife, Rose Scarscelli, was born in Clarksburg, West Virginia. She was a kind little Italian lady who worked hard all her life as a homemaker and raised seven children."

One of those children was James, the only one of Rose's children to leave Clarksburg.

"Dad was born on April 28, 1933 in Clarksburg," Jimmy noted. "He joined the Navy in 1951 at age 18 and spent three years traveling around the world and eventually was discharged in San Francisco. Dad was a bit of a rouge and was always getting into fights. He liked to box and had a temper when provoked."

James once got into a fight when his ship was docked in Hawaii.

"Dad was a cook in the Navy," Jimmy explained:

> That's where he learned to cook for masses of folks. The first night his ship docked in Hawaii he had just cleaned up the mess hall and closed the kitchen when a Marine shows up and demands dinner. Dad told him the galley was closed but the Marine persisted, and Dad and he ended up going at it. As a result, Dad was thrown in the brig for fighting and never got off the ship. He only saw Hawaii from a porthole.

After he was discharged, James returned to Clarksburg and started a restaurant there.

"His nickname at the time was 'Chickles,'" Jimmy laughed:

James Lopez during his days in the U.S. Navy, which set the stage for him opening a variety of Springfield eateries, beginning with the first Taco Bell east of the Mississippi River in 1968. (*Jimmy Lopez photo*)

> He started this little beer joint that served great hot dogs. Dad was very resourceful and made do with what he had. He bought his first stove out of a junk yard. In the meantime, Mom's [Edith Vogt] sister [Louise Vogt] had married a GI from Clarksburg who was stationed in Germany. Mom was born in 1928 and raised in Frankfurt, Germany and had decided to visit the United States to see her sister. She was a little scared about coming to America but soon got over that. Louise and her husband took Mom to eat at Dad's beer joint on a Friday night and Dad saw her and asked her out on a date for the following Friday.
>
> That next Friday, Mom shows up at the beer joint ready for her date and Dad says to her "I'm sorry but I can't go out, my help didn't show up." Mom looks at him and says, "give me an apron and I'll be your help." They worked together every day since then until the day they both passed. I never saw them fight or argue and that was amazing since they worked together side by side for all those years.

James and Edith were married in Clarksburg in 1957, but James had an itch to move west. The confines of Clarksburg were too much for the experienced navy cook who had seen the world.

"Dad had grown weary of the small-town mentality," Jimmy said:

> He didn't like the fact that everybody knew everybody else's business. So, he and mom sold the beer joint to his sister, Thelma DeFazio, and her son still sells hot dogs there. Dad had wanted to go back to California ever since he left the service but had felt obligated to return home. Now, he wanted to start a new life and a family. He and

James and Edith Lopez (center and right) at the couple's 1957 wedding. (*Jimmy Lopez photo*)

> Mom opened a restaurant called the East Gate Café on El Cahone Blvd in San Diego. They served plate lunches with Mom waiting tables and Dad cooking.
>
> Taco Bell was just starting to branch out with franchises and Dad inquired about it. Their restaurant was doing well—almost too well in that they were so busy they never had a free moment.

Jimmy was born in 1960 and his sister, Nancy, followed in 1963, and James and Edith wanted their children to grow up in a Midwestern environment.

"Dad worked alongside (Taco Bell founder) Glenn Bell for two weeks, learning the rungs of the company ladder before buying a franchise in San Diego," Jimmy continued. "He used that Taco Bell to get his feet wet, and when an opportunity arose for him to purchase the first promotional store in Springfield, Dad traded the San Diego restaurant for the Springfield location."

The Lopez family packed their bags and headed east, landing at 2056 Prospect Circle, just a block north of the Taco Bell location on Main and Douglas Streets.

"Dad picked that location to live because he said if something happened to his car he could always walk to work and that's what he did most of the time," Jimmy remembered.

At the time, there were no Mexican restaurants in or around Springfield. Lopez's restaurant was the 270th of the Torrance, California, Taco Bell chain, located at 2050 East Main Street, at the corner of Douglas Street. With its mission architectural lines, the building was erected for $80,000 and featured five main items of tacos, burritos, tostadas, frijoles, and "bell burgers."

Right: Acknowledgement letter from Taco Bell in June 1968 of James Lopez' purchase of the Springfield restaurant. (*Jimmy Lopez photo*)

Below: The opening of James Lopez's (left) Taco Bell restaurant on Main Street took place with Perla Aquirre, Miss Mexico 1968 (second from left); Louisa Flook, Miss Springfield 1968 (third from right); Glenn Bell, Taco Bell CEO (second from right); and Dave Broderick, Taco Bell East Coast Franchise Chairman (right) in attendance along with Lopez. (*Jimmy Lopez photo*)

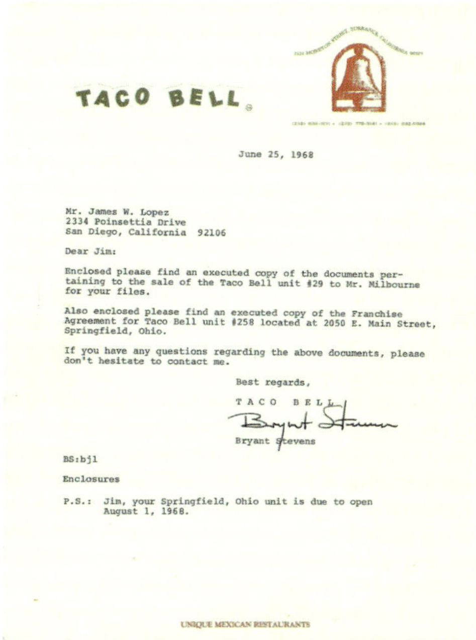

TACO BELL®

June 25, 1968

Mr. James W. Lopez
2334 Poinsettia Drive
San Diego, California 92106

Dear Jim:

Enclosed please find an executed copy of the documents pertaining to the sale of the Taco Bell unit #29 to Mr. Milbourne for your files.

Also enclosed please find an executed copy of the Franchise Agreement for Taco Bell unit #258 located at 2050 E. Main Street, Springfield, Ohio.

If you have any questions regarding the above documents, please don't hesitate to contact me.

Best regards,

TACO BELL

Bryant Stevens

BS:bjl

Enclosures

P.S.: Jim, your Springfield, Ohio unit is due to open August 1, 1968.

UNIQUE MEXICAN RESTAURANTS

"Nobody knew what Mexican food was," Jimmy said:

People didn't know anything about it. What grew the business was the kids—the kids tried it because everything in the restaurant cost 25 cents or less. The business took off and from 1968 to 1975 was very profitable. Dad did everything and in seven years only had 14 days off. He had two days off a year—Thanksgiving and Christmas—and quite honestly, didn't have them off as he was cooking for family.

Dad was starting to get burned out and he had Mom and myself and Nancy all working there. At the end of 1975 he started putting chili on the menu and Mom added some potted plants around the restaurant for homier feel and put up some framed Mexican money on the walls. One day a corporate guy from Taco Bell walks in and "says you can't have chili on the menu or plants in the restaurant or framed Mexican money on the walls." The guy also had a scale and told Dad he was being too generous with his portions. But that was Dad—his burritos and tacos were over-flowing, and his portions were always hefty.

James Lopez's Taco Bell on Main Street was consistently packed with customers and was a favorite with Springfield teenagers. James was never shy, providing patrons with hefty portions of ingredients in his tasty tacos. (*Jimmy Lopez photo*)

James had to give Taco Bell corporate 7 percent of every dollar he made, Jimmy said.

"Mom and Dad were tired and talked about retiring," Jimmy noted. "So, they decided to sell the Taco Bell and open a small mom and pop place. Dad bought a small place near the Fairfax Motel on Main Street, and as soon as local folks learned Dad was back in the kitchen, the new place took off."

Christened "Jim's Coney Island," the new restaurant also had a drive-through. James and Edith ran the restaurant while Jimmy and Nancy operated the drive-through.

"Dad was great at starting businesses from the ground up and once they got super successful, he wanted to move on to a new project," Jimmy said. "But he had a heart attack in 1982, and kind of lost his drive for new projects. He was always go, go, go and it finally caught up with him. He later sold Jim's Coney Island and retired."

In 1985, James purchased the small strip of buildings where "Big Jim's" now stands. Jimmy has been running the uber-popular diner located at 1928 Mitchell Boulevard since 2007.

"It's a challenge but I love it," Jimmy said. "We have a lot of loyal customers and I try to be kind to people and follow in the footsteps of my father by serving generous portions of quality food at reasonable prices."

James Lopez, Sr., a friend to many in Springfield, with his warm smile, generous heart, and signature mustache, passed away on July 29, 2015.[1]

12

Springfield Sports Notables

Dave Burba

Dave Burba, born on July 7, 1966, became a Major League Baseball pitcher with the Seattle Mariners, San Francisco Giants, Cincinnati Reds, Cleveland Indians, Texas Rangers, and Milwaukee Brewers from 1990 to 2004. Born in Dayton and raised in Springfield, Burba went to Kenton Ridge High School and The Ohio State University, making his MLB debut as right-handed thrower on September 8, 1990 for the Seattle Mariners. His fifteen-year career saw him score a 115:87 win/loss record, with 1,398 strikeouts and a 4.49 ERA.

After his MLB days were over in 2011, Burba began his pitching coach career, first with the Tri-City Dust Devils and later with the Modesto Nuts (2013–2014); the New Britain Rock Cats (2015); the Yartford Yard Goats (2016–2017); and with the Lancaster JetHawks (2018–2019). Burba's uncle, Ray Hathaway, a Greenville, Ohio, native, had pitched four games for the Brooklyn Dodgers in 1945 as a twenty-eight-year-old right-handed rookie.

Adam Eaton

Adam Corey Eaton was born on December 6, 1988 in Springfield and became a Major League baseball player first for the Arizona Diamondbacks (2012–2013), the Chicago White Sox (2014–2016), and currently as an outfielder for the Washington Nationals (2017 to present).

After graduating from Kenton Ridge High School—where he excelled as both a pitcher and an outfielder and led his team to regional finals (2004 and 2005)—Eaton attended Miami University on a basketball scholarship. He was chosen in the nineteenth round of the 2010 Major League draft and scored a .340 batting average with the Diamondback's minor league teams in 2010 and 2011; he was named Pioneer League All-Star Outfielder (2010) and California League All-Star (2011).

Eaton was called up to the majors on September 4, 2012 and made his debut in July 2013, starting in sixty-six games that first season. Later that year, he was traded to the Chicago

Above left: Dave Burba attended Kenton Ridge High School and The Ohio State University before becoming a successful Major League baseball pitcher. (*Don Rinker photo*)

Above right: Adam Eaton is another Kenton Ridge alumnus who went on to have great success in the Major Leagues, playing for the Chicago White Sox and the 2019 World Series Champions Washington Nationals. (*Author photo*)

Right: Adam Eaton's Washington National baseball card. (*Author photo*)

White Sox, batting .300 during the 2014 season in the Windy City, signing a five-year contract worth $23.5 million. The White Sox then traded Eaton on December 7, 2016 to the Washington Nationals for three players. Plagued with injuries, Eaton nevertheless compiled a .301 average in 2018. Just a year later, Eaton hit a homerun in Game Two of the World Series, as the Nationals bested the Houston Astros for the 2019 Championship.

Harvey Haddix

Harvey Haddix was a Major League pitcher who was born in Springfield on September 18, 1925; he spent his early years on his family's 450-acre farm, throwing a ball against the steps of the family home. He began pitching in high school, and at the age of seventeen, he attended a tryout in Columbus for a spot on the St. Louis Cardinals team. On the scouting form, he wrote down that he was a "pitcher, catcher and outfielder," and was told that he had to pick one, so he chose pitcher, throwing twelve southpaw pitches for a Cardinal's scout. He signed with the Cardinals in 1947 and was given the moniker "The Kitten" for his resemblance to their pitching ace Harry "The Cat" Brecheen.

Haddix played with the Cardinals (1952–1956), Philadelphia Phillies (1956–1957), Cincinnati Reds (1958), Pittsburg Pirates (1959–1963), and Baltimore Orioles (1964–1965).

He is best known for pitching a twelve-inning no hitter for the Pirates on May 26, 1959, retiring thirty-six consecutive batters in twelve innings via his signature fastball and slider. The Pirates ultimately lost to the Milwaukee Braves in the thirteenth inning, 1:0, but the then thirty-three-year-old's performance before 19,194 fans in Milwaukee County Municipal Stadium is considered by many to be one of the best games ever pitched.

Haddix's 1953 season with St. Louis was his finest as he compiled a 20:9 record with 163 strikeouts and a 3.06 ERA, with nineteen complete games and six shutouts. He helped garner the Pirates a victory in the 1960 World Series as the winning pitcher of Game Seven as a reliever when the Pirates won the game in the bottom of the ninth inning off Bill Mazeroski's walk-off homerun.

Haddix retired in 1965 and spent the next fourteen years as a pitching coach for the Reds, Mets, Red Sox, Indians, and Pirates. He retired as a three-time All Star (1953, 1954, 1955); three-time Golden Glove Award winner (1958, 1959, 1960); and was co-player of the month for May 1959. He holds the record for the most consecutive batters retired in one game (thirty-six). Haddix Field, a little league baseball park in New Carlisle, Ohio, is named in his honor. He passed away on January 8, 1994 at the age of sixty-eight from emphysema.

Alice Hohlmayer

Alice "Lefty" Hohlmayer was one of the original members of the All-American Girls Professional Baseball League from 1943 to 1954. Born on January 19, 1925 in Springfield, Lefty was the daughter of Carl and Marguerite Hohlmayer. Her father was the local milkman and laundromat owner and her mother was a homemaker. Lefty began her career in sports at the age of five, playing softball with her brothers, and

Above left: Harvey Haddix was first signed by the St. Louis Cardinals in 1947. (*Don Rinker photo*)

Above right: Haddix is best known for pitching a near no-hitter in twelve innings against the Pirates on May 26, 1959, and later played for the Pittsburg-based Major League team. (*Don Rinker photo*)

she got her nickname due to her left-handed hitting and throwing prowess. She played first base in the 1937 All-Star Team at the state tournament and excelled in other sports such as basketball, field hockey, tennis, and volleyball. After graduating from Springfield High School in 1942, she enrolled at The Ohio State University, where she was discovered by a talent scout in 1945 and signed by the Kenosha Comets a year later.

Lefty was a strong-hitting left-handed pitcher who was on first base when not on the pitcher's mound. In 1948, she pitched forty-two consecutive scoreless innings playing for the Kenosha Comets (1946–1948), and later played for the Muskegon Lassies (1949), Kalamazoo Lassies (1950), and Peoria Redwings (1950–1951). She played in a total of 486 Major League games, with 1,486 at bats, with eighty-five runs, 301 hits (35-2B; 15-3B), 128 RBIs, with a .203 average. As a thrower, she had a 35:32 win/loss record from eighty-nine games, with a .508 percentage from 579 innings pitched. Listed at 5 feet 6 inches and 160 pounds, she graduated from Ohio State with a Bachelor of Arts in physical education and health in 1949.

Upon retirement from her professional career, Lefty taught sixth and seventh grades and worked for the Fairfield, California, Recreation Department for seventeen years.

Alice "Lefty" Hohlmayer is the only female member of the Springfield Baseball Hall of Fame. (*Don Rinker photo*)

She was the only woman who played in the "55 years and older" World Men's Slow Pitch Tournament in Las Vegas in 1981 and once got a hit off Satchel Paige in an All-Star Game. She passed away in 2017 at the age of ninety-two in Bonita, California.

Ray Lucas

Ray Wesley Lucas was a Major League right-handed pitcher and minor league baseball scout and manager. Born on October 2, 1908 in Springfield, Lucas pitched for the New York Giants and the Brooklyn Dodgers over the course of five seasons. He compiled a 1:1 record from twenty-two games, with one save and an ERA of 5.79.

As a hitter, Lucas had three hits in nine tries, for a .333 batting average. He was unable to play baseball after his hand was shot off accidently while hunting. He died on October 10, 1969 in Harrison, Michigan at the age of sixty-one.

Davey Moore

Boxing great Davey (David Schultz) Moore, born on November 1, 1933 in Lexington, was known as the "Springfield Rifle" for his ties to the Champion City. He was raised in Springfield and went to Kiefer Junior High and Springfield High School before making his professional boxing debut at the age of nineteen against Willie Reece, winning in the sixth round on May 11, 1953. He also served on the 1952 U.S. Olympic Team as a bantamweight amateur. He captured the World Featherweight Championship title on

Above left: Ray Lucas was born and raised in Springfield and played for the New York Giants. (*Don Rinker photo*)

Above right: Boxing great Davey Moore had thirty knockouts to his credit before his untimely death on March 23, 1963. (*Author photo*)

March 18, 1959 from Hogan "Kid" Bassey and went on to defend his title five times afterward, with a career fifty-nine wins, seven loses, one draw, and one no contest.

Thirty of Moore's triumphs came by knockout. However, on March 21, 1963, he suffered injuries that resulted in his demise on March 25, 1963. During an intense match against Ultiminio "Sugar" Ramos, Moore suffered such severe head injuries that he was never able to recover. The fight was so brutal that Moore's manager, Willie Ketchum, stopped the fight in the tenth round, when it was supposed to go a full fifteen rounds. The fight was shown on national television before an audience of 22,000.

Despite the pounding Moore endured, he was lively and animated afterward, telling reporters "Look, you guys know when I'm right nothing gets to me. Not nothing. I was off. That's it plain and simple." Ten minutes later, Moore was screaming in pain, calling Ketchum "My head, Willie! My head! It hurts something awful!"

Rushed into White Memorial Hospital, Moore was near comatose and died soon after. His passing caused eruptions within the boxing world, with proposed bans on pugilistic contests running rampant through legislative circles. On September 21, 2013—the fiftieth anniversary year of Moore's final fight—the city of Springfield dedicated an 8-foot bronze statue of Moore near his former home. More than 250 people attended the ceremony, including Sugar Ramos, who flew in from Mexico to pay his respects to his fallen competitor, as well as Moore's widow, Geraldine Moore.

William Mosconi

William Mosconi—one of the most famous names in twentieth-century American professional pool—scored a coup at the East High Billiard Club in Springfield on March 19 and 20, 1954 when he set a world record by running 526 consecutive balls without a miss during an exhibition. Mosconi, known to all as "Mr. Pocket Billiards," won thirteen World Straight Pool Championships between 1941 and 1956 and was one of the first to be inducted into the Billiard Congress of American Hall of Fame in 1968 at the age of fifty-five. He is credited for bringing the sport of pool to national attention and was a consultant on the 1961 film *The Hustler*, which starred Paul Newman, George C. Scott, and Jackie Gleason, among others.

13

Artists, Celebrities, & Musicians

Berenice Alice Abbot

Berenice Alice Abbot was a celebrated portrait and architecture (1930s) and scientific (1940–1960) photographer. Born on July 17, 1898 to Lillian Alice Bunn and Charles E. Abbott, she was raised in Springfield by her divorced mother and attended The Ohio State University. She left college after only two semesters and moved to Europe where she studied sculpture in both Paris and Berlin. She became smitten with photography as well as poetry after she was hired by Man Ray as a darkroom assistant in his Paris Montparnasse studio. “I took to photography like a duck to water,” she later wrote. “I never wanted to do anything else.”

Abbot’s first photography exhibition came at Le Sacre du Printemps gallery in 1926, and she later had her own studios on Rue du Bac and Rue Servandoni. She often chose figures in the literary world for her portraits, including Jean Cocteau and James Joyce. After visiting New York City in 1929, she decided to relocate and focus on photographing the city. Her work became a chronological reference for many of the city’s lost buildings and neighborhoods, and it mirrored the development of the industrial revolution and urban planning of Manhattan. She lived for more than four decades in Greenwich Village with her partner and art critic Elizabeth McCausland, who wrote routinely for the *Springfield Daily Republican*.

William Burnett

William Riley (W. R.) Burnett was born on November 25, 1899 in Springfield, residing in his hometown until the age of twenty-five, when he relocated to Chicago. Before moving to the Windy City, Burnett had written more than 100 short stories and five novels but had not sought out a publisher. Chicago proved to be a turning point for Burnett, who took a job as a night clerk at the six-story Northmere Hotel, 4943 N. Kenmore Ave, a spot on the city’s far northwest side. At the time, the area was frequented by less desirables such as gangsters, thieves, prostitutes, and hustlers.

Left: Springfield native Bernice Abbot became a world-renowned photographer and is especially noted for her black and white portraits of New York City. (*Hank O'Neal photo*)

Below: A Bernice Abbot photograph of New York City. (*Author photo*)

William Burnett was an author turned screenwriter who hit it big in Hollywood with such films as *Little Caesar*, *High Sierra*, and *The Great Escape*, among others. (*Author photo*)

Immersed in this world, Burnett thus had his inspiration for his 1929 novel *Little Caesar*. This brought him overnight success and sent Hollywood calling on his doorstep. He was hired by First National Pictures (Warner Brothers) as a screenwriter, with a film by the same name becoming reality in 1931, starring Edward G. Robinson. He won the 1930 O. Henry Award for the short story *Dressing Up*, which appeared in a November 1929 edition of *Harper's Weekly*; he was also the screenwriter behind *Scarface* in 1932. Burnett's other works as a screenwriter include *High Sierra* (1941), *Wake Island* (1942 Oscar Nominee), and *The Asphalt Jungle* (1949). He also earned a Writer's Guild Award nomination for penning *The Great Escape* (1963).

Garvin Bushell

Garvin Bushell, born on September 25, 1902, was one of many talented, multi-instrumental jazz musicians to hail from the Champion City. A student of both classical and jazz, he plied his wares on the clarinet, alto clarinet, oboe, English horn, flute, saxophone, bassoon, and contrabassoon. Some of those jazz artists he collaborated with include Perry Bradford, Chick Webb, Fletcher Henderson, Bunk Johnson, Fats Waller, Cab Calloway, Eric Dolphy, Gil Evans, and John Coltrane. He began playing piano at the age of six before playing clarinet in a 1916 circus band; he moved to New York to perform with Harlem cabarets in 1919, and he played with Mamie Smith's Jazz Hounds after studying classical music at Wilberforce University. He eventually landed a gig with the Sam Wooding Ensemble—one of the first black jazz bands to perform in Europe, Russia, and South America from 1925 to 1927.

Springfield native and talented musician Garvin Bushell's *One Steady Roll* album cover. (*Author photo*)

In his book *Jazz from the Beginning* (University of Michigan Press, 1988), Bushell recalls vividly on some of the personalities he worked alongside, and the racial prejudice he experienced both at home and abroad. He was a member of the Louisiana Sugar Babes Quartet (with James Johnson, Fats Waller, and Jabbo Smith), becoming one of the first recorded jazz bassoonists in 1928. He later became a music teacher, while playing bassoon with the Chicago Civic Orchestra, and he was part of both the Fletcher Henderson Reunion Band and the Wilbur DeParis' New Orleans Jazz Band in the late 1950s and early 1960s. Bushell passed away on October 31, 1991 after a lengthy career that ran from jazz's early age until nearly the time of his death, when he was working as woodwind instructor in Las Vegas.

Godfrey Frankenstein

One of the first artists to call Springfield home, Godfrey Frankenstein emigrated to the United States with his parents and to Cincinnati in 1931, where he began working for a sign painter at the age of twelve. The following year, he opened his own painting business, and seven years later, he relocated to Springfield, where he began painting pictures of Buck Creek and the Mad River.

As a youngster, Frankenstein had been fascinated with painting and paint in general, learning to mix his colors using pig blood (for red), coffee (for yellows), and a mixture of ink and water (for grays and shadows). After morphing from a sign painter into a *bona fide* and respected landscape artist, he would spend twenty-two years painting a panoramic portrait of Niagara Falls followed by a two-year stint traveling through and painting scenes of Europe. Upon his return to the United States, he relocated to Springfield where he died aged fifty-two. The last painting he worked on was entitled *Mad River, Fern Cliffs*.

One of painter Godfrey Frankenstein's many scenes of Clark County, this one entitled *Mad River Near Springfield.* (*Author photo*)

LILLIAN GISH

"The First Lady of the Silent Screen," Lillian Diana Gish was born on October 14, 1893 to Mary Robinson McConnell Gish and James Leigh Gish—former Urbana, Ohio, residents. In fact, Lillian emerged into this world the same year Thomas Edison created the motion picture. Along with her sister, Dorothy, Gish became an iconic figure in cinematic history, and the two-story house on 621 Linden Street where she and her family resided still stands today. When Dorothy was born on March 11, 1898, the family moved to Dayton and on to Baltimore, where James partnered in an ill-fated candy store. He abandoned his family soon after, leaving his wife and daughters to fend for themselves. Mary soon joined a stock company and took the girls to New York City, where stage opportunities for children were many. She rented an apartment on West 34th Street, and Lillian made her stage debut at the age of nine in *Convict's Stripes*, earning $10 a week.

Mary, Lillian, and Dorothy all became hired by separate touring groups during the first decade of the twentieth century. It was in 1905 that Lillian became friends with Gladys Smith, another child stage star like herself. Four years later, Lillian and Dorothy were watching a short silent film, *Lena & The Geese*, when they recognized Gladys as the star of the movie. In 1910, the sisters went to the Biograph Film Studios at 11 East 14th Street to visit their friend, who had changed her name to Mary Pickford.

Pickford introduced them to famed silent director D. W. Griffith, who was producing multiple films on a weekly basis. In a rehearsal hall, he began shooting a gun over the two girls' heads to garner their reaction. "We didn't realize it was an audition," Lillian related, and went on to make forty movies with the famed director, including *The Birth of a Nation* (1915), *Intolerance* (1916), *Way Down East* (1920), and *Orphans of the*

Above left: Lillian Gish, born in Springfield on October 14, 1893, became known as the "First Lady of the Silent Screen." (*Author photo*)

Above right: This ad, which appeared in the *Springfield Daily News* in early September 1916, was for the new Lillian Gish film *Annie Laurie* that was debuting at Springfield's Majestic Theater. (*Clark County Historical Society Archives*)

Storm (1922). She was nominated twice for an Academy Award in the same category—for Best Supporting Actress in 1946's *Duel in the Sun* and 1967's *The Comedians*, and she was awarded an Honorary Oscar in 1971. She made movies in eight decades and performed for eighty-five years on screen, stage, and television. Lillian passed away at the age of ninety-nine on February 27, 1993 in New York City, leaving the bulk of her fortune to friend and fellow actress Helen Hayes.

Griffin House

Griffin House is another in a long line of Springfield natives whose musical endeavors have led him to national prominence. Inspired by such greats as Bruce Springsteen and Woody Guthrie, House, who was born April 21, 1980, grew up modestly. His father worked in a tire shop while his mother found foster families for children in need. Though he had a scholarship to Ohio University, he chose instead to attend Miami University in Oxford, and it was there that he embraced his musical talents. Upon graduation, he moved to Nashville, working on his first album, *Upland*, which debuted in 2003.

Nine albums later, House continues to record and perform his mix of blues, Americana, and adult mix with such musicians as John Mellencamp, Patti Scialfa, The

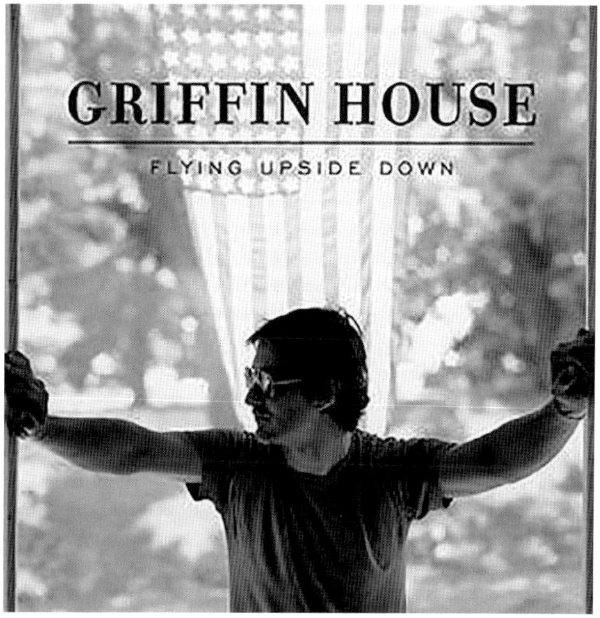

Griffin House continues to be a Springfield favorite. His album *Flying Upside Down*, shown here, was released October 9, 2007. (*Author photo*)

Cranberries, Josh Ritter, and Mat Kearney. Many of House's lyrics reflect experiences from his Springfield upbringing.

Quentin Jackson

Quentin Jackson was Duke Ellington's top trombonist from 1949–1960, known primarily for his "wa-wa" sounds. Growing up in Springfield, Jackson had been taught to play the trombone by his brother-in-law, Claude Jones, a member of McKinney's Cotton Pickers; with him, Jackson would later tour in 1931. Throughout his career, Jackson toured and played with such top artists as Cab Calloway (1940–1948) and the Don Redman Orchestra (1932–1940), where he was also a ballad singer. After leaving Ellington, he toured with Quincy Jones in 1960 before performing with Count Basie from 1961–1962 before returning to Ellington in 1963. In the early to mid-1970s, he performed with the Thad Jones/Mel Lewis orchestra.

Bradley Kincaid

Though born in Bluegrass State, the name Bradley Kincaid is synonymous with music in Springfield. Born in Point Leavell, Kentucky, on July 13, 1895, Kincaid was one of the most celebrated country artists of the first half of the twentieth century. Hailing from the wilds of Appalachia, Kincaid's first musical prize was a treasured guitar that his father had procured after trading a family foxhound for the instrument. When Kincaid's mother died in 1909 and his father abandoned the children, Kincaid was raised by his older sister, hoping to find a way out of the country life via his treasured guitar, which he christened "Houn Dawg."

Kincaid's foray into the music industry took a twisted path, as after serving in the army for two years during World War I, he returned to school, graduating from Berea High School in 1921 at the age of twenty-six. One year later, he married his music teacher, Irma Foreman, and moved to Chicago in 1926, where a solo audition on National Barn Dance on the Windy City's popular WLS radio station led to a permanent spot on the program. Billed as "the Kentucky Mountain Boy," Kincaid received thousands of fan mail every week, and went on to record every year through 1950, with his thirteen songbooks selling nearly a million copies. He was the first country artist to publish a songbook and was known for popularizing traditional county folk songs, especially "Barbara Allen," "Red River Valley," "On Top of Old Smoky," etc. Kincaid broadcasted throughout America, with his last gig at the Grand Ole Opry on WSM in Nashville (1946–1950).

He retired and settled in Springfield in late 1950s, buying an interest in WYSO and a music store located inside the Arcade. He was inducted into the Nashville Songwriter's Hall of Fame in 1971, and today, Kincaid's Music (located on Front Street) is a Springfield mainstay, with many in the community having walked through its doors. Kincaid remained active until his passing, aged ninety-two, on September 23, 1989.

ADA LEE

Ada Lee had the pedigree to be a top musician, as her father was a professional trumpeter and her mother was a pianist, organist, and singer. Born in Springfield in the early 1930s, she began recording and performing jazz, blues, gospel, and soul throughout North America in the late 1950s. She began singing in junior high school and studying voice as a teenager, both with teachers in Springfield and at the Dayton Conservatory of Music, focusing on classical, jazz, and popular music of the day. Eventually, she landed a singing gig with Springfield's Bus Palmer Band, performing on the weekends and appearing on southwestern Ohio's radio programs and singing with Dayton and Cincinnati bands. That led to a musical scholarship to Wilberforce University after she performed on WHIO-TV's *Wendy Berrie Talent Show*.

Upon graduation, she sang with both Count Basie and Lionel Hampton and soon nabbed bookings at both the Apollo Theater in New York City and at The Flame Show Bar in Detroit. When she sang at the 1960 Buffalo Jazz Festival, organizer George Wein booked her for future shows and became her personal manager. One year later, *Billboard* magazine awarded her album four stars, stating: "Ada Lee is a young thrush with a warm and interesting voice, making her debut disking with this release. She comes off mighty well too, due to a good selection of tunes, bright vocal work and attractive arrangements by conductor Dick Hyman. Good wax."

She moved to Toronto in 1967 where she met and married her husband, Frank Barker, and raised six children in a nearby suburb of Peterborough, where they became one of the first interracial families in the area.

"We were like the Brady Bunch," she later remarked "We didn't feel entirely welcome at first. A neighbor circulated a petition to try to get us to move away, thinking that

Right: Known as the "Kentucky Mountain Boy," Bradly Kincaid became a name synonymous with music in Springfield. (*Author photo*)

Below: A fantastic collection of Bradly Kincaid's best music for the dedicated country and rockabilly enthusiast. (*Author photo*)

Ada Lee album back cover from the early 1960s. (*Author photo*)

having a black person next door would decrease property values. They didn't realize I had run around with Ella Fitzgerald and Sarah Vaughn."

JOHNNY LYTLE

Johnny (John Dillard) Lytle was born on October 13, 1932 in Springfield, and though he passed away on December 15, 1995 in his hometown, he is still considered to be one of the best "vibes" players ever. In fact, Lionel Hampton referred to Lytle as "the greatest vibes player in the world." Over the six decades that he recorded and performed, he produced more than thirty jazz records for labels such as Tuba, Jazzland, Solid State, and Muse.

Lytle—the son of an organist mother and trumpeter father—certainly had the pedigree to be an outstanding musician and began playing the piano and drums before the age of nine, performing with his father's band as the drummer at that young age.

Prior to devoting himself to music full-time, he became a Golden Gloves champion, but his quest for music prevailed and he turned his passion into a successful career. He began performing with Ray Charles, Jimmy Witherspoon, and Gene Ammonds as a drummer in the late 1950s and then, inspired by the Lionel Hampton, began performing on the vibraphone (a vibraphone is a member of the percussion family consisting of tuned metal bars and is played by holding two to four soft mallets and striking the bars). He started his own jazz band in 1957 with drummer William "Peppy" Hinnant, saxophonist Boots Johnson, and organist Milton Harris, and together, this group recorded for Riverside Records under the direction of Orrin Keepnews, a Grammy Award-winning producer.

This Johnny Lytle album cover featured one of the best "vibe" players in this history of Jazz. Lytle, born and raised in Springfield, developed a unique style that has yet to be rivaled. (*Author photo*)

"He would play because he just loved playing," Barbara Lytle, his wife of four decades, told *Springfield News-Sun* staffer Andrew McGinn in an October 27, 2009 article. "We weren't rich, but we weren't poor either. I was happy with it."

Coined early on his career with the title "Fast Hands," Lytle scored chart-topped albums with *Lika A Groove*, *The Loop*, and *Moon Child*, recording his own hits (as a songwriter) such as "The Village Caller," "The Loop," "The Man," "Lela," and others. He recorded and performed with many of jazz's greatest, including Louis Armstrong, Miles Davis, Roy Ayers, Bobby Timmons, and Hampton throughout North America and Europe. A big admirer of Miles Davis, Lytle wrote the tune "Selim" (Miles spelled backwards) as an homage to Davis. A father of three, Lytle was accompanied by his son, Marcel, on several of his records as both a drummer and a vocalist.

The devoted father and family man always managed to find time for his community amid his constant touring and performing that continued well into the 1970s, '80s, and '90s. He last performed in his hometown with the Springfield Symphony Orchestra on November 18, 1995 at the Kuss Auditorium. He passed away just a little less than a month later at the age of sixty-three from liver failure. He had recently signed on to the Muse label to begin recording a new CD. Besides his wife, Barbara, he left behind two sons, Marcel and Michael, and a daughter, Ayo Michelle. After his passing, the street where he lived was renamed "Johnny Lytle Avenue."

William McKinney

William B. McKinney formed the first modern Big Band of the Swing era, McKinney's Cotton Pickers in Springfield in 1923, as the band's manager, after a successful career as

William McKinney album cover featuring McKinney's Cotton Pickers. (*Author photo*)

a circus drummer. Born on September 17, 1895 in Cynthiana, Kentucky, McKinney was known for his fast-playing rhythms and heart-stopping beats.

Originally christened the Synco Septet Jazz Band, the Cotton Pickers performed regularly throughout the Midwest and were considered the best of the rival bands of Duke Ellington and Fletcher Henderson. Their most famous gig was at Frank Sebastian's Cotton Club in Culver City, California, where they performed in May 1931. They were also one of the first African American bands to play on national radio, and they continued performing throughout the U.S. into the late 1930s. McKinney died on October 14, 1969.

Minnie Miller

Minnie Willis Baines Miller was an acclaimed author and Springfield resident for most of her life. Known mainly for works championing women's rights and issues, she was born on January 8, 1845 in Lebanon, New Hampshire, to Horace F. and Minerva Tisdale Willis. Her family moved to Springfield when she was quite young, and she excelled in both composition and poetry in her early years before receiving her master's degree from Wittenberg.

Her first writing exposés were in *Waverly* magazine when she was just fourteen years old, with her bestsellers *The Silent Land* (1890), *His Cousin, The Doctor* (1891), *The Pilgrim's Visions* (1892), and *Mrs. Cherry's Sister* (1900) all coming later. She was also a frequent contributor to local religious newspapers and journals and was the first president of the Springfield Woman's Pioneer Press Club—an organization for women writers.

Author Winnie Willis Baines Miller was a lifelong Springfield resident who championed women's rights in most of her writings. (*Clark County Historical Society Archives*)

Clarence Phillips

Clarence Coles Phillips was an artist born and raised in Springfield who became well known for the illustrations he created for advertisements and magazine covers. Born on October 3, 1880, Phillips was the son of Anna Seys and Jacob Phillips. He attended Kenyon College from 1902 to 1904, with his first published watercolor illustrations appearing in the Kenyon yearbook *The Reveille* those years.

After college, he moved to New York City and opened his own advertising agency, employing, among others, a young Edward Hopper—one of his former classmates at Kenyon. After a chance meeting with J. A. Mitchell, publisher of *Life* magazine, Phillips was hired and began a career at the age of twenty-six that enshrined him with readers through his "fadeaway" images—a figure whose clothing morphed into the background of the image.

This would become Phillip's mantra throughout his career, and his works were popular with readers and advertisers alike. He produced covers for numerous magazines besides *Life*, including *Good Housekeeping*, and for companies such as Holeproof Hosiery, Oneida Community dinnerware, and the U.S. Naval Academy Yearbook. He died aged forty-seven in 1927 from kidney failure.

Cecil Scott

Born in Springfield on November 5, 1905, Cecil Scott was an accomplished clarinetist, tenor saxophonist, and jazz bandleader. In his early years, he often played alongside his brother, drummer Lloyd Scott, and in the 1920s, the pair and a group of other notable musicians took up residency in New York's famed Savoy Ballroom. In the 1930s, he took up with bassist Ellsworth Reynolds and then with Teddy Hill and later with the pianist Teddy Wilson's orchestra.

Above left: Springfield native Clarence Phillips was an artist famed for his "fade-away" images. (*Clark County Historical Society Archives*)

Above right: A fade-away painting by artist Clarence Phillips. (*Author's photo*)

Above left: Cecil Scott, who worked with many jazz and swing bands from the 1920s through the 1960s, at work. (*Nat Goodwin photo*)

Above right: The "Springfield Stomp" recording by Cecil Scott on the Victor 78 recording label. (*Author photo*)

Scott is noted for serving as backup to Billie Holiday's finest recordings and performed with jazz and swing greats such as Henry "Red" Allen and Willie "The Lion" Smith. Scott is credited on more than seventy-five albums and is credited as the leader of the Washboard Band, which produced the hit "Springfield Stomp" on the Victor label. Scott passed away on January 5, 1964 in New York City.

Sir Charles Thompson

Springfield native Sir Charles Thompson was a well-known instrumentalist whose first musical inclination was the violin before switching to jazz piano as a teenager. He started working with local bands in the 1930s and preferred the smaller bands and clubs, utilizing a light-fingered technique he garnered from Count Basie, which eventually morphed into the style of music known then as "bop." He picked up this technique while studying the works and working with such artists as Lionel Hampton, Fletcher Henderson, Jimmy Dorsey, and the great Count Basie himself.

After performing in small clubs in New York City during World War II, Thompson found himself in Hollywood, recording bop for Capitol Records with the Coleman Hawkins/Howard McGhee band. His classic works include "Ladies' Lullaby" and "Robbins' Nest." Though he spent a good portion of his career touring as a freelance organist throughout North American, Europe, and Canada, Thompson continued to record group albums in the 1950s and 1960s, for labels such as Vanguard, Columbia, and Apollo.

Tommy Tucker

Tommy Tucker (a.k.a. Robert Higginbotham) was born on March 5, 1933 to Leroy and Mary Higginbotham, the fifth of eleven children, and became a well-known jazz singer-songwriter and blues pianist. His 1964 song "Hi-Heel Sneakers" sold more than 1 million copies and became eleventh on the *Billboard* Hot 100 chart and was twenty-third on the U.K. Singles Chart.

As a teenager, he became an amateur prize fighter before turning his attention to music full-time, traveling and performing in the United States and Europe with the likes of Ray Charles and Dionne Warwick. He passed away unexpectedly in 1982, aged forty-eight.

Earle Warren

Earle Warren was born on July 1, 1914 in Springfield and after spending time in the Midwest with his family's band, he became Count Basie's go-to alto saxophonist and ballad singer, beginning in 1937. He also played piano, ukulele, and banjo.

Warren played in Alan Freed's December 1959 *Christmas Jubilee* and was featured in the 1970 film *Born to Swing*. In his later years, Warren split his time between the West End Jazz Club (on 116th and Broadway) in New York City and Switzerland, leading a band called The Countsmen, which featured former Basie band members trombonist Dicky Wells and bassist Peck Morrison. He died on June 4, 1994.

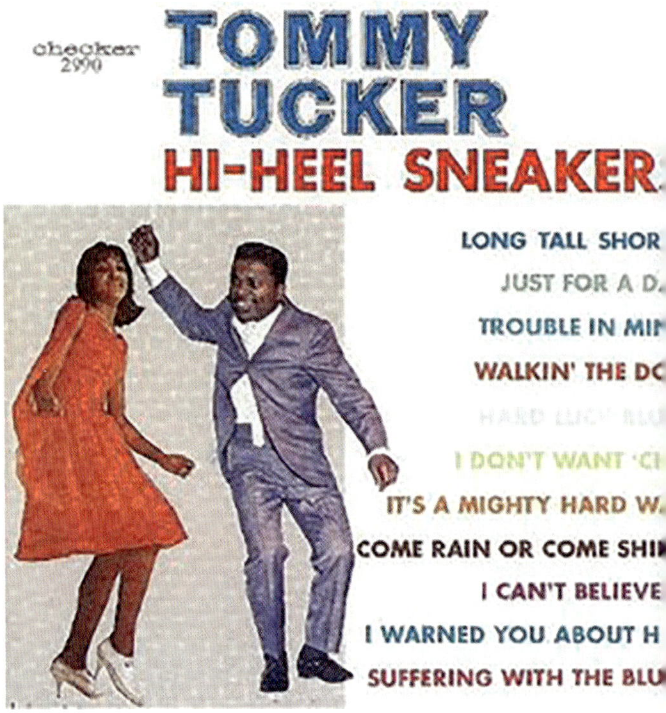

Above left: Sir Charles Thompson was a Springfield native whose musical talents included violin and piano. (*Author photo*)

Above right: Tommy Tucker album cover featuring the jazz singer's hit *Hi-Heel Sneakers*. (*Author photo*)

Left: Springfield native Earle Warren was a member of Count Basie's band. (*Clark County Historical Society Archives)*

14

The Wild & Wacky Mr. Winters

The name Johnathan Winters is synonymous with the early days of radio, television, and comedy. Born Johnathan Harshman Winters III on November 11, 1925 in Dayton, Ohio, he was the son of a banker and investment broker and grandson of the Valentine Winters, founder of Dayton's Winters National Bank. His mother was Alice Kilgore Rodgers, a Springfield radio personality whose family was of English and Scotch-Irish ancestry.

"Mother and Dad didn't understand me, and I didn't understand them," he quipped to Jim Lehrer in 1999. "It was a strange kind of arrangement."

When the family's money was drained by the Great Depression, his parents divorced in 1932 and Winters went with his mother to live at his grandmother's Springfield home. Winters' mother worked in the Crowell-Collier factor and hosted a women's radio program on WIZE-AM. The young Winters frequented the Regent and other local movie houses, obsessed with film, once telling a reporter in 1985 that the 1933 motion picture *King Kong* "made the biggest impression on me as a youngster."

During his senior year at Springfield High School, aged seventeen, Winters enlisted in the Marine Corps and served as a gunner on an aircraft carrier for two years in the Pacific. He later enrolled in Kenyon College and the Dayton Art Institute before meeting and marrying Eileen Schauder in 1948, whom he remained with until her death on January 11, 2009. Their son, Jay, is a contractor and their daughter, Lucinda, is a movie talent scout.

In a July 30, 2011 edition of NPR's *Weekend Edition*, Winters lamented over his childhood and his parents. "They were both insanely jealous of my career," he said, stating that he was often lonely and that his parents often belittled him and mostly ignored him. He recalled when he took his mother, Alice (then Bahman), onto *The Jack Paar Tonight Show*, thinking she would enjoy the opportunity. "Jack said, 'You got a hell of a talent here,'" Winters recalled. "'You must be very proud of him.' And my mother said, 'He's the biggest joke I ever wrote.'"

The bitterness Winters felt carried over into personal demons that would emerge later in life, forcing him to self-institutionalize after battling alcoholism and two nervous breakdowns—the first in 1959 and the second in 1961. He had admitted being an alcoholic in his younger days, following in the footsteps of his father. Most often, he cited his mother as his comedic mentor.

He soon landed a spot as a morning D.J. at WING, and made up guests to appear on his show; he told *US News & World Report* in 1988: "I'd make up people like Dr. Hardbody of the Atomic Energy Commission or an Englishman whose blimp had crash-landed in Dayton." He appeared with his mother on CBS's 1952 show *I've Got a Secret*, and through 1953, he hosted numerous programs for WBNS-TV before moving to New York City in 1954 with just $56 in his pocket. Living with friends in Greenwich Village, Winters performed in nightclubs, using characters he had invented in his radio days in his stand-up routine, and often doing impressions of Cary Grant, Groucho Marx, John Wayne, and James Cagney.

In a 1997 *Orange County Register* interview, Winters said an audience member from those early New York stand-up days told him: "What's the matter with those characters in Ohio? I'll bet there are some far-out dudes that you grew up with back in Ohio." Thus began his practice of using folks from his Springfield roots in the creation of his characters. Maude Frickert and Elwood P. Suggins—two of his most infamous characters—were based on people Winters had met during his youth in Springfield. Winters said Maude Frickert was inspired by an old aunt who taught him to drink and play poker as a nine-year-old. Winters told *US News & World Report*: "As a kid, I wanted to be a lot of things. I was a Walter Mitty type. I wanted to be in the French Foreign Legion, a detective, a doctor, a test pilot with a scarf, a fisherman who hauled in a tremendous marlin after a 12-hour fight."

"There were a number of characters growing up that were like this," he told a reporter in his later years. "I thought many times I wanted to come back (to Ohio), especially after my wife died. I mean, outside of the weather, that's about all you've got here. I would come back in a minute. But (with) my luck, I'd come out of some condominium or apartment and fall on the snow and never get up."

Soon, he appeared as "Johnny Winters" on the TV show *Chance of a Lifetime* with host Dennis James and eventually garnered his own weekly, fifteen-minute TV series, *The Jonathan Winters Show*. In 1956, he became the first person to be broadcast in color, and in 1960, he received a star on the Hollywood Walk of Fame.

Through 1964, Winters worked as a voice-over for TV commercials, specifically for Utica Club beer, providing the voices of Shultz and Dooley, a pair of beer steins. Later, he was the spokesperson for Hefty trash bags, appearing as both his popular "Maude Frickert" character and others. He made a national impression in 1964, appearing on *The Jack Paar Tonight Show* as a trio of personalities including a lion tamer, bullfighter, fisherman, and musician, prompting Paar to coin him as "pound for pound, the funniest man alive."

The Jonathan Winter's Show was expanded in 1967 to 1969 to an hour-long variety show and continued as *The Wacky World of Jonathan Winters* from 1972 to 1974. Despite his success, he never strayed far from Springfield.

One day in the mid-'70s, he strolled into Meek's Sporting Goods.

"He just walked into the store and of course everyone recognized him right away," said Meek's owner, Don Rinker. "He wanted me to make a Springfield High School jacket for him, which we did, and which he later wore on *The Tonight Show with Johnny Carson*."

This photo shows Jonathan Winters standing in the Meek's Sporting Goods' gun department with owner Don Rinker (left) and the comedian's longtime friend Harry Poulin (right), a classmate of Winters at Springfield High School. An unnamed Meek's employee and Catholic Central High School student stands behind the trio. (*Don Rinker photo*)

Winters earned his first Grammy for his work on the 1975 album *The Little Prince*, and twenty-one years later, he won a second for his work on the 1996 comedy album *Crank Calls*. In 1981, he starred on *Mork & Mindy* as the son of Robin William's Mork and his earth wife in that popular TV show's final season.

In 1984, he performed live onstage at Memorial Hall for the Springfield Arts Council during the same time he was a regular on the television program *Hee Haw*. Later that decade, he was the voice of Grandpa Smurf on the TV series *The Smurfs*. He went on to do voice-overs for several TV series and movies for the next two decades. He won an Emmy for Outstanding Actor in a Comedy Series for his portrayal of eccentric grandfather Gunny Davis in *Davis Rules*, a 1991 and 1992 TV series. Several years later, he gave one of his few straight performances as uncle and stern police chief to Alec Baldwin's Lamont Cranston in the film *The Shadow*. He was awarded the Kennedy Center's Mark Twain Prize for Humor in 1999.

Winters died of natural causes on April 11, 2013 at the age of eighty-seven at his home in Montecito, California; he is survived by his two children, Lucinda and Jay, and five grandchildren.

15

How Sweet It Is

Growing up, Alicia Sweet never dreamed she would be following in the footsteps of her father W. Dean Sweet, the founder of agricultural giant Sweet Manufacturing, located on Springfield's east side at 2000 Leffel Lane.

"I never aspired to take over, as my older brother Alan was already involved in manufacturing and engineering," Alicia stated. "When I was a senior business major at Wittenberg, I had a break from Thanksgiving to New Year and was approached by Bob Riser, the president of Sweet at the time who asked if I was interested in working as they were short-staffed in advertising and sales."

Alicia worked that Christmas break and graduated in May 1982. Her father was chairman of the board.

"Mr. Riser contacted me and asked if I had any plans after graduation," Alicia offered. "My dream was to go to a big city like Chicago and work for an ad agency. But Mr. Riser said he had an entry level position in advertising, and I thought it would be a good way for me to get experience and grow my wings."

"I worked there about eight weeks and then the farm markets became depressed," she continued:

> Farms were having hardships with grain prices and a lot of framers were losing their farms. I got laid off. When that happened, folks were shocked since I was a family member of a family-owned business. But later there was an opening in purchasing and I was hired back and worked in that department before going back to advertising and sales and eventually to accounting. I was controller, then general manager and in 1996 became president of the company.

"I loved every step of the process and it seemed like a natural progression," Alicia continued. "For me, it made the business puzzle pieces fit together that produced the outcome for the customer. So, it made sense that I learned every facet of the business."

Alicia's father, Dean, was a graduate of Springfield High School and served as the Wildcat mascot during his years there, where he was friends with Jonathon Winters, among many others. His father, Walter Sweet, was Springfield's chief of police from

Alicia Sweet, President and CEO of Sweet Manufacturing. (*Alicia Sweet photo*)

1950 to 1952 and later the chief of police at Cedar Point. After graduating from The Ohio State University, Dean worked to bring his vision of innovation within the galvanized bucket elevator industry to fruition, and Sweet Manufacturing was born in November 1955.

"Dad ran Drake Manufacturing after the owner had passed away and the widow asked him to run the business for a year," Alicia explained:

> Dad saw the need for that type of the maternal handling equipment in the marketplace and saw that it could be done in a more efficient way. His goal was to produce a quality product with a longer life and he figured out how to do that in a cost-effective way.
>
> When the widow decided to discontinue the business, Dad asked three Drake employees if they wanted to start a new business with him, and he bought the Crabill Airport and re-designed the equipment, and that's how the company started in November of 1955. The location was excellent because it was right near Interstate 70.

Growing up, Alicia was featured in early advertisements touting the "Sweetheart" elevator buckets with the moniker "Miss Sweet."

> All I knew was that my Dad ran this company and he used us three kids to do his mass direct mailings. He brought home boxes of catalogues and pre-printed envelopes and

Springfield's former Crabil Airport, now the site of Sweet Manufacturing. (*Alicia Sweet photo*)

> we had to stuff the envelopes and lick the envelopes and he paid us a penny a piece. My two brothers, Alan, Roger and I had to do this. That kind of set the stage for our future.
>
> My dad was very clever about how he provided opportunities for his employees' growth. He did it in a subtle way, saying to an individual "I want you to go over here and try this." He had an instinct about where a person was best suited for a spot but wouldn't tell them. He would just kind of throw it out there and let them figure it out.

Sweet Manufacturing has expanded and evolved over the decades, serving both the North American and International markets. Today, the Sweet name is found in fifty-five countries on six continents, serving a plethora of agricultural industry giants. Much of that growth can be directly traced to Alicia's perseverance and foresight, but it was not always an easy road.

"There were very few women in any position whatsoever in the agricultural industry," she noted:

> I first noticed there was a gender deficiency in 1996 when I was asked to serve on the Board of Directors for the American Feed Industry Association. It was a 42-member Board and I was one of only three women on that board and we were referred to as 'the skirts.' That attitude has changed in today's environment and I think it was just a matter of holding your ground and being yourself and proving that you're their equal in knowledge and work ethic.

Alicia's father Dean was honored in 1998, 2005, and 2009 with the prestigious Ohio Governor's Excellence in Exporting Award, recognizing his accomplishments in the exporting industry and the impact Sweet Manufacturing brought to the Ohio economy.

"When Dad developed the business, he designed his own product line and incorporated needs and improvements in the industry that would help fuel the demand for his product and it took off," Alicia acknowledged. "In the industry, he's known as the pioneer of galvanized material handling equipment."

Alicia explained that during the first five years Sweet Manufacturing was in operation, Dean produced equipment that was fabricated in black iron material, which had to be primed and painted:

> Dad thought that [priming and painting] added a lot of indirect labor to a product that then has to be maintained over the years. So, his concept was to produce all-galvanized steel equipment, so it didn't have to be painted or maintained, and it has a much longer life.
>
> Today it seems like common sense, but he had that insight to think about the customer's needs long before anyone else did so. He wanted to minimize the upkeep of the product and that's how he came up with the trademark name, Silver Sweet, for our bucket elevators.[1]

Alicia is proud of carrying the family business begun by her father seven decades ago to new heights. She is a testament to how Springfield has evolved in 219 years and is a terrific role model for young woman seeking prominent positions in Clark County's business environment.

W. Dean Sweet, founder of Sweet Manufacturing. (*Alicia Sweet photo*)

16

Final Thoughts

When I first undertook writing this book, I had no idea of Springfield's vast, fascinating history. A small group of history aficionados provided insight that otherwise would have been missed—foremost Natalie Fritz at the Springfield Heritage Center, who offered her expertise in locating photos, newspapers, and materials found within this manuscript.

As well, I cannot thank enough members of the Ronemus and Baylor families and Jimmie and Lindy Lough, as well as North High School classmates and longtime friends Jimmy Lopez and Alicia Sweet for sharing their stories.

Finally, I thank the most important person in my life, my father, Don Rinker, whose ever-uplifting view of life, people, and animals has inspired me to treat all of God's beings with respect and kindness.

Thanks for giving me a great life, Dad, I'll see ya a little further upstream.

The author and her parents, Ginger and Don Rinker, and nephew, Kyle Rinker, after winning a harness race with her pacer Magic Wand at Springfield's Fairgrounds on July 27, 1992. Harness racing was discontinued at the Clark County Fair several years later. (*Brad Conrad photo*)

Endnotes

Chapter 2

1 Rowell, *American Newspaper Directory, Part 1*, (1873) p. 178.
2 *New York Times*, May 27, 1924, p. 1.

Chapter 4

1 *New York Times*, February 28, 1906, p. 1.
2 Heer, *Black Readers & White Comics*, *The Comic's Journal*, April 7, 2011.

Chapter 5

1 *FBI.gov*, Famous Cases.
2 Stockton, *Allthatsinteresting.com, John Dillinger Wasn't Just A Bank Robber,* July 13, 2019.
3 *Springfield News,* September 22, 1933, p. 1.

Chapter 6

1 *New York Times,* January 16, 1904, p. 7.
2 *Los Angele Times,* October 25, 1923, p. 1.
3 *Blackmailers Enter Pleas of Guilty, Cincinnati Enquirer,* October 31, 1923, p. 1.
4 *Los Angeles Examiner*, March 30, 1924, p. 2.

Chapter 7

1 Rinker, K., Interview with Donald Rinker, 2019.

Chapter 8

1 Rinker, K., Interview with Jimmie and Lindy Lough, 2019.

Chapter 9

1 Rinker, K., Interview with Kyle Ronemus & Mike Ronemus, 2019.

Chapter 10

1 Ronemus, N., *Memoirs of Julie Heaume*, 2019.

Chapter 11

1 Rinker, K., Interview with Jimmy Lopez, 2019.

Chapter 15

1 Rinker, K., Interview with Alicia Sweet, 2019.

Bibliography

Books

Bushell, G., *Jazz from the Beginning* (Ann Arbor: University of Michigan Press, 1989)

Crumb, R., *Heroes of Blues, Jazz & Country* (New York: Abrams Comicarts, 1994)

Embry, W., *The Inside Game, Race, Power & Politics in the NBA* (Akron: University of Akron Press, 2004)

Freedman, L., *Hard-Luck Harvey Haddix and the Greatest Game Every Lost* (Jefferson, North Carolina: McFarland Publishing, 2009)

Gilman, A., *American People; a complete history of the United States* (Springfield: Mast, Crowell & Kirkpatrick, 1895)

Gish, L., *The Movies, Mr. Griffith, and Me* (New York: Prentice Hall Publishing, 1969)

Howard, M. K., *Black Lynching in the Promised Land: Mob Violence in Ohio, 1877-1916* (Columbus: Columbus State Community College, 2017)

Kinnison, W. A., *Wittenberg in Clark County, 1845-1970* (Springfield: Clark County Historical Society, 1970)

Mann. J., *Tinseltown: Murder, Morphine & Madness at the dawn of* Hollywood (New York: Harper, 2014)

Prince, B. F., *Standard History of Springfield & Clark County; an authentic narrative of the past* (Chicago & New York: The American History Society, 1922)

Rockel, W. M., *20th Century History of Springfield, and Clark County, Ohio* (Biographical Publishing Co., Chicago, 1908)

S.A.B.R., *Society for American Baseball Research*, (SABR.com, 2019)

Steele, A., *The History of Clark County, Ohio* (Chicago: Oscar Martin & W. H. Beers & Co, 1881)

Turner, E. I., *It Happened in Springfield* (Springfield: Springfield Tribune Printing Company, 1958)

Magazines and Newspapers

Cincinnati Enquirer, p. 1, Cincinnati, Ohio, American Security & Trust Company, October 31, 1923

Collier's, The National Weekly, cover, New York City, New York, Crowell Publishing Company, January 21, 1922

Los Angeles Examiner, p. 2, Los Angeles, California, William Randolph Hearst, March 30, 1924

Los Angele Times, p. 1, Los Angeles, California, Harry Chandler, October 24, 1923

New York Times, p. 7, New York City, New York, Adolph Ochs, January 16, 1904

New York Times, p. 1, New York City, New York, Adolph Ochs, February 28, 1906

New York Times, p. 1, New York Times, New York, Adolph Ochs, May 27, 1924
Springfield Daily News, p. 1, p. 3, Springfield, Ohio, Press Republic Company, June 11, 1916
Springfield Daily News, p. 7, Springfield, Ohio, Press Republic Company, June 13, 1916
Springfield Daily News, p. 1, Springfield, Ohio, Press Republic Company, August 4, 1917
Springfield Daily News, p. 16, Springfield, Ohio, Press Republic Company, September 15, 1927
Springfield Daily News, p. 1, Springfield, Ohio, Press Republic Company, September 22, 1933
Springfield Daily News, p. 1, Springfield, Ohio, Press Republic Company, August 18, 1948
Springfield Daily Republic, p. 3, Springfield, Ohio, John M. Gallagher, June 23, 1881
Springfield Globe Republic, p. 1, Springfield, Ohio, John M. Gallagher, July 15, 1881
Sports Illustrated, cover, New York City, New York, theMaven Inc., November 3, 1975
Time Magazine, cover, New York City, New York, Time Inc., May 1, 2017
The Comic's Journal, p. 1, Seattle, Washington, Fantagraphic Books, Inc., April 7, 2011
The Springfield Post, pp. 1, 6, Springfield, Ohio, Ben-Teau Publishing, May 17, July 19, 1956

INTERVIEWS

Rinker, K., Interview with Jimmy Lopez (Springfield, Ohio, 2019)
Rinker, K., Interview with Jimmie and Lindy Lough (Springfield, Ohio, 2019)
Rinker, K., Interview with Donald Rinker (Springfield, Ohio, 2019)
Rinker, K., Interview with Kyle Ronemus (Springfield, Ohio, 2019)
Rinker, K., Interview with Mike Ronemus (Springfield, Ohio, 2019)
Rinker, K., Interview with Alicia Sweet (Springfield, Ohio, 2019)